VIRGO

2005

Cover Design: Sam Grimmer

Published in 2004 by Hinkler Books Pty Ltd
17–23 Redwood Drive
Dingley VIC 3172 Australia
www.hinklerbooks.com

© Hinkler Books Pty Ltd 2004
Reprinted 2004

All rights reserved. No part of this publication may be reproduced, stored in a retrieval system, or transmitted in any way or by any means, electronic, mechanical, photocopying, recording or otherwise, without the prior written permission of the copyright holders.

ISBN 1 7412 1558 7
Printed and bound in Australia

CONTENTS

PART 1
INTRODUCTION 1
- History 2
- How Horoscopes are Written 3
- How Reliable are they? 4

PART 2
THE YEAR 2005 5
- Yearly Overview 5

YOUR DAILY GUIDE 8
- January 8
- February 15
- March 22
- April 30
- May 37
- June 44
- July 51
- August 58
- September 65
- October 72
- November 79
- December 85

PART 3
THE VIRGO SUN SIGN 93
- The Virgo Character 93
- Famous Virgo Sun Signs 97
- Sun Sign Compatibility 99
- Other Compatibilities 145

INTRODUCTION

Welcome to the astonishing, intriguing world of horoscopes in astrology. The year 2005 promises to be exciting across all the signs. I hope to navigate you safely through the coming months with some words of wisdom and insight. Consider this little book a road map to a successful and fulfilling year!

Consulting 'the stars' when making decisions is a time-honoured tradition. The American Indians, the South American Inca, the Australian Aborigines and many ancient cultures have looked up into the night sky and given meaning to the turnings of the great astral wheels above them.

Astrology is a science of observation. That is, it is a process developed over thousands of years of observations of the stars and the influence their placement has over all manner of earthly phenomena. Police have observed that a full moon will mean a busy night at the police station. Gardeners have observed that it is better to tend certain vegetables at certain phases of the moon. And meteorologists have observed that longer weather patterns, such as El Nino, can be predicted by the stars.

This guide to your daily horoscopes for 2005 is an extension of that tradition. By looking at the night sky and taking your sun sign into account, it is possible to make predictions about what sort of a year 2005 will be for you.

Part 1 of this book provides a brief history of astrology. I also explain how I made the predictions contained in the day-by-day guide in the second part of the book.

Part 2 gives you the day-by-day guide to the year, with an overview covering the main things that will happen to you in the important areas of relationships, career and money, and health.

Part 3 of the book provide a comprehensive outline of the characteristics of the Virgo sun sign and a full list of your compatibilities with other sun signs.

I wish you the very best in 2005 and hope this book plays some part in your coming successes.

HISTORY

Most historians and astrologers agree that astrology can be traced back to Babylonia (now Iraq) about 3500 years ago, in the first half of the Hammurabi dynasty. The Babylonians, noted for their advanced culture, had a well-developed science of observational astronomy. This provided them with a complex calendar to use for times to plant and harvest, times to hold religious festivals and so on.

Each planet was given importance, and the priests named the planets in honour of their many gods, such as Ishtar, now known as the planet Venus, and Nergal, now known as Mars. By about 1000 BC, the Babylonians had developed a sense of 'planetary omens' and put their minds to setting their system down in literature.

Since Nergal was the god of war, when this planet shone brightly in the sky, the Babylonians took it as a sign that it was a good time to wage war. As Ishtar was the goddess of love, a spring night in which that planet shone high in the west after sunset was considered a good time for romance. This was the first basic horoscope.

It is interesting to note that across the seas in South America, the Incas had also given the same meanings to each planet. This happened even though the two societies grew up independently of each other until the Spanish 'discovered' South America in 1532!

By 600 BC, the Babylonians had devised the twelve-sign zodiac by developing markers in the sky that corresponded roughly to the months of the year. This is when the concept of making predictions based on the signs began to develop and became more complex. Eventually, the Babylonians were able to make a map of the heavens to use in divination.

INTRODUCTION

The oldest horoscope that has been discovered dates to 29 April 410 BC, when it is known that horoscope predictions were extremely popular.

In later centuries, the popularity of astrology waned. By 1900, a French encyclopaedia was describing it as 'a vanishing cult', with 'no young devotees'.

Then came a revival. Astrology bounced back, leading to the remarkable passion and devotion people have for it today. The catalyst was British astrologer RH Naylor who, after World War I, invented the daily newspaper astrology column. It attracted many readers, and now there is barely a newspaper or magazine on the planet that does not publish a regular horoscope.

In these astrological charts, people found a form of self-reflection that they were not finding elsewhere in their lives. The result is that now 90 per cent of all Americans under the age of thirty know their sun sign, and there are more than 10,000 practising astrologers in the United States.

Millions of dollars are spent annually in Australia, the United States and Europe by people consulting astrologers. The Emperor Caligula, Claudius, Ptolemy, St Augustine, Queen Elizabeth I and more recent figures, such as former US president Ronald Reagan and Princess Diana, have all looked to the stars for guidance.

Looks like the Babylonians were on to a good thing!

HOW HOROSCOPES ARE WRITTEN

To come up with your daily horoscope, I have taken the chart of each day (using the Equal House System) and turned the zodiac wheel so that zero degrees of your sign Virgo sits on the ascendant. I take a note of the relationships of your ruling planet (in Virgo's case this is Mercury) and make some rough predictions.

I then look at the planet that rules the sign that Mercury is in at the time of the reading. This planet is called the dispositor, and I make more-detailed assertions from where it sits in relation to Mercury.

When a house contains a lot of planetary energy, this means that aspects of your life will be focussed in that area. I make notes on whether this is easy or difficult energy. Significant events in the heavens, such as when two planets align, are also noted. If a day's energy is particularly significant for your sign, it has been highlighted.

The moon also plays a leading role in any horoscope, so a special note is made of new and full moons.

HOW RELIABLE ARE THEY?

It would be fair to ask at this point, how can we make daily predictions for all the people born in one particular month? Humans are a diverse bunch with different interests and different lifestyles, so how can we categorise people's experiences into only twelve separate boxes?

The problem is in the variables. Each planet, each sign and each house has several different meanings, and it is possible I have chosen the one that is not relevant to you. All the same, the issues are generally similar, so you will get a good idea of how it applies in your situation. As with anything in this world, nothing beats common sense.

There can be no doubting the horoscope's worth in giving people another way to look at a situation, or inspiring them to great things. I hope this book can give you a whole new perspective on a problem that has been troubling you, and provide a framework within which you can look for the meaning in your life.

THE YEAR 2005

YEARLY OVERVIEW

The year 2005 begins as it ends – surrounded by family and concerned with the home. In fact, there is likely to be an event involving your family in the first week of the year.

You can really win with your words around 10 January, which coincides with the new Moon, so be sure to kick start your New Year's resolutions with conviction. The spotlight is on money and material matters for Virgo this year – you can shop 'til you drop and you won't mind one bit!

Your energy levels are concentrated towards your family until mid-February, after which you will be ready for a bit of fun. Your party sector is energised until late March, when work will become a priority. Your finances will be highlighted from mid-June to August. And for the last five months of the year, your energy reserves will be concentrated on improving your education.

RELATIONSHIPS

Romance features early in the year for Virgo, as Venus enters your lurve sector on 9 January. This is the beginning of a month of joy and fun. There is certain to be lots of invitations to parties and you'll receive plenty of attention until mid-February. You are really shining and you'll be great fun to be around, with lots of energy for friends and flirting.

This might see you delighting in a delectable fling. Your heart won't really be in it, as work will get in the way, so this romance is unlikely to go the full distance. It is an important building block, though, as it will increase your confidence and get you feeling good about yourself.

It might also shine a light in a dark corner and encourage you to expand your horizons a little. Perhaps you will realise that your tastes have been too restrictive and that your perfect partner won't necessarily come packaged exactly as you would like.

Consolidating serious possibilities will happen in late February. For those of you in an established partnership, this will be a great time to get married or renew a commitment to each other, as your mind will be clear and your feelings focused on each other.

CAREER AND MONEY

This is your year for luck in your money and spending sector, and you'll be feeling pretty benevolent for most of the year. Extravagant gift giving will be a feature of 2005 and you will find joy in buying thoughtful presents for your loved ones.

Mid-March could be a stressful time for money, when a major financial undertaking turns sour. You could have bitten off more than you can chew at this time.

You have abundant energy for making money as well as spending it in September. If you're not slogging it out at work, you'll be in the shops spending the spoils of your labour.

HEALTH

You should guard against eschewing the treadmill for TV and chocolate biscuits in the New Year. Comfort is very attractive at the beginning of 2005 and it will take a great deal of concerted effort to stick to your New Year's resolutions, but you can pat yourself on the back if you do.

You start feeling energised in February and have plenty of juice in the tank for lots of activities, but they will be mostly of the party, party, party type, so try limit the champagne and canapes. If you took your health and fitness for granted and overindulged a little too much over the Christmas break, you might find you're feeling a little sluggish by now.

Fortunately, Mars comes along to kick you out of your chair in late March and you will think about starting a fitness program, joining a gym or signing up for a class of some sort. You should have no trouble motivating yourself at this time

YOUR DAILY GUIDE

Saturday 1 January
You will feel neither here nor there when it comes to your personal goals, except for those that are work related. This failure to set goals is resulting in a lack of clear direction and focus of energy. You must set targets if you want to achieve anything that is worthwhile in your eyes. You can't pretend to have the same aims as other people just to satisfy yourself that you have direction in life.

Sunday 2 January
You will find inspiration from unknown sources today, but there could be a loss if you push your luck too far. Try to keep your head above the chaos to keep from going off track and losing valuable ground in a difficult project. Finding energy and confidence when dealing with your children might be a problem as you are distracted.

Monday 3 January
As the Moon wanes to its last quarter in the sky, wrap up the final details on your assignment. Dot the i's and cross the t's to make sure your efforts have maximum effect. Mercury, Venus and Pluto are indulging in a mènage à trois in your home sector today, so watch out for an argument that could change everything. There is also the possibility of a romantic encounter on the domestic front.

Tuesday 4 January
You will find yourself forced to make important decisions, but seizing control of your destiny has always been something that others seem to find important but you have never really seen the need. You are a child of the universe

YOUR DAILY GUIDE

and you don't need to call the shots to know you will be well looked after, but you may find that you are starting to enjoy your own feelings of control and that your actions are making a difference, however small.

Wednesday 5 January
Today you will intuit the needs of others. In fact, when you watch a person you will feel as if their thoughts are words written in the air. Some will be happy to use this to their advantage, especially in an intense meeting of minds where the true intent of each person is carefully veiled. For maximum effect you will have to temporarily turn off your ability to empathise because this will lead you into a conflict of desires.

Thursday 6 January
You will find yourself on the receiving end of someone else's problems if your perception fails to identify those who are clingy and dependent on others. While you may in fact let someone down, you might prefer to hold yourself over for bigger fish in the sea. Be wary of those offering easy rewards with methods that seem too good to be true.

Friday 7 January
You will be well complemented by your friends who present you as witty and intelligent. This helps you impress a few people who would never give you the time of day. While you are more able to get your point of view across, don't expect it to be embraced. There may be some trouble with your phone lines today or your email access at work could be playing up.

Saturday 8 January
You are afraid of being stuck in an emotional rut, so if you get a chance to do something a little different or a little exciting, you won't regret it. You have to give yourself space to work through repressed emotions about a recent

loss. Hopefully your partner or lover will be able to sense your situation and schedule a little rest and resuscitation.

Sunday 9 January

Committing yourself to hard work is the key to success, but what kind of success will depend on what kind of work. When solving a problem, consider all aspects of the situation thoroughly, rather than summing everything up in one sweep of the eye and coming to a quick conclusion. Sometimes you are better to rely on a trusty calculator than expose yourself to errors with creative guesswork.

Monday 10 January

The Moon is stirring the sky and this brings an opportunity for you at work. Make the most of it, but be prepared to devote the next month to your idea. Today you are benefiting from an increase in your communication skills and a strong and attractive physical presence at work. Use your spunky vibe to your advantage and get the tide drifting your way.

Tuesday 11 January

You struggle with the perception that you are distant, but at least you are finding a sense of beauty in the idea of a hidden self. Assume that friends see parts of you that you don't want to know about but that you should probably open your eyes to. You are feeling more emotionally secure in a partnership than you have been over the past couple of days and it is a good time to solidify bonds.

Wednesday 12 January

Your energy is pointed in the direction of possessions and your communication is pointed towards social groups, so this could have some interesting consequences. Perhaps you would be best organising a tupperware party, or a charity ball to take advantage of this fortuitous aspect? You are in contact with both your energy and your communication skills in a very obvious, conscious way that will enable you to dictate the terms.

YOUR DAILY GUIDE

Thursday 13 January
Your energy will not let you down if you attempt to bite off more than you can chew. Things are going very well in business or in your relationship because of your effective communication. People are finding you to be a very warm person and a pleasure to deal with, so you should not try to analyse your success too much but enjoy it while you can.

Friday 14 January
Those with business acumen are able to make connections and strike balances more than other career seekers right now. In general, however, friends will be absolutely invaluable. Tonight, the stars catch you in a mesmerising dance of romance, or romantic delusion, from which escape is unthinkable. You may be inclined to drift between the pages of fact and fiction, so beware of losing ground recently made through good decisions.

Saturday 15 January
Have faith in yourself as a teacher while there is a willing student, as you are in great shape to lead from the front. Take the time to look at yourself holistically and you will learn to pass on your wisdom to others who are having trouble finding their own way. Mental blocks might seem to be a hindrance at first, until you realise how much higher you get when you stack a few together.

Sunday 16 January
This month you will be focussing on relationships and you will have a lot of energy for this area. Conversations and communications will keep you on your toes, so establish what your short-term plans are before you to commit to anything that requires discipline and reliability. It's a bad time for group projects, so put them on hold for a while and stick to enjoying yourself rather than getting ambitious.

VIRGO · 2005

Monday 17 January
As the Moon waxes to half in the sky, your efforts towards your social life should be well under way. Remember, well begun is half-done. Although you are progressive in your attitudes to relationships in general, you have lagged behind in your attitude to the relationship you are in. You should be more attentive when the pressure of work and social commitments is high, and perhaps that cuts both ways.

Tuesday 18 January
A period has come to an end where the wonders of the universe were closed to your mind. Limitless possibilities come back to tease you, and you see that your life energy ebbs and flows like the tides. Your world has been motoring along a very conservative path for the past couple of months, and it has been particularly frustrating for forward thinkers around you.

Wednesday 19 January
You will have no problem motivating yourself to most challenges today. But you might prefer to use your energy for good rather than to serve your own ends. Some will call on you to solve problems that seem worthy on the surface, but don't expect too much altruism today. Find someone who doesn't ask for help and offer them your support – you might find real satisfaction in this.

Thursday 20 January
The Sun has moved into your work sector and this month you will find yourself with renewed energy to get many of the jobs done that have been left undone for too long. Your industrious mood means you will be able to really push through and tick off some things on your list both at work and in the home. Don't waste this time on details. Just move on the projects that have been really weighing on your mind.

YOUR DAILY GUIDE

Friday 21 January
Turning the tables on animosity is about taking the first step in reconciliation, just don't expose yourself to betrayal. As for the tensions you feel between yourself and work colleagues – ride them out as long as you can because the face that confronts yours over the partition will change eventually. Manage your personality clashes like you would manage a Bengal tiger

Saturday 22 January
When a friend comes to you with a revelation that embarrasses you, your first instinct is to run for cover. Take a moment to think things through and you will realise that a minor misunderstanding is the cause of it. You won't be content to accept anything without question, which is a little problem between you and your friends that has gone on long enough. A family outing may have to be cancelled.

Sunday 23 January
It is a highly perceptive time for you and details will be brought into clear focus. It is important that you do not lose your grip on your temper when you see or intuit more than other people expect you too. It might be a good time to work out whether or not you are going to achieve some unrealistic goals you set for yourself earlier in the year. Maybe the opportunity has come to transfer the effort to other things.

Monday 24 January
Your beguiling nature of the past few days continues – use it. Strong emotions in the area of material gains could make for some nasty situations – just remember what your mama said and the Beatles added to – it is only money and money can't buy love. You win some you lose some, and all those cliches and truisms are so-called because behind every cliche there is a nugget of truth.

VIRGO · 2005

Tuesday 25 January
Progress towards your lunar goal should be reaching its zenith today with the appearance of a full Moon. Take advantage of its abundant energies to push forward. There are more important things to deal with than what you may or may not get out of the present situation. Keep your mind open to the idea that your present path might leave you dissatisfied and wishing for a different outcome.

Wednesday 26 January
You sometimes dream of a world where all people are united in their quest to live in harmony. Sounds pretty good, hey? However, your comforts and emotional well-being suggest that you are more likely to serve your immediate needs, which often doesn't include others. An erratic mood swing may change your mind about a commitment you've made in your career – hold off on any action for now.

Thursday 27 January
You sometimes wonder whether you would ever have come this far in your career without a spouse or close friend supporting you. Sometimes you rely on mental stimulation when the deep wells of your inspiration threaten to dry up. A wide range of experiences and even some forgettable failures have allowed you to consolidate your knowledge into good solid rules for success. Keep your eyes on the prize.

Friday 28 January
An interesting day for you lies ahead as Mars aligns with Pluto in your family sector. Your energy meets the potential for significant change, so whatever happens, it will be of your own divination. It could be as simple as deciding to go on a family holiday, or as life-changing as deciding to move home. Whatever it is, make your decision responsibly.

YOUR DAILY GUIDE

Saturday 29 January
Your imagination is peaking in ways you are not normally accustomed to. Be wary of taking a few shortcuts today, especially when it comes to communicating with a wider group or anything to do with your hobbies and entertainment, as you could undo yourself. Your voice is as smooth as honey, but you may not be taking as much time to think through the things you say.

Sunday 30 January
As Mercury joins the Sun in your work sector, you will find your ability to think clearly about your industrious goals is increased. Be wise about what you plan and how much you expect to achieve, because although your capacity to enjoy life will be high, your ability to realise complex outcomes will be virtually nonexistent.

Monday 31 January
You may find yourself singled out for blame in a situation that is not really your fault, but rather a problem with a wider group of people with which you are typically associated. For example, a protest for a cause that you believe in could turn ugly, and even if you weren't there, you will be asked to explain yourself to friends and family. A situation that returns to haunt you again and again will be resolved if you put in the effort.

Tuesday 1 February
You are finding it hard to make strong and balanced one-on-one connections with people who you have little in common with. Not surprising really, but you could really do with a break at the moment. Bide your time in the background and life will pass you by, so you need to make some bold decisions. Maybe the best approach is to use your guile and sex appeal.

Wednesday 2 February
As the Moon wanes to darkness in the sky, you should be wrapping up the final details on your lunar goal.

VIRGO · 2005

Remember to tie up any of the loose ends that could bring you undone. You have a number of things that you want to achieve, but you think that dreaming of success and building game plans in your mind will help you get of the couch and into the driver's seat.

Thursday 3 February

As Venus moves into your work sector, you will find beauty in getting your hands dirty. Although you are working through your limitations, this is proving to be rewarding while it continues to open up new areas of your life and potential. You'll be given an opportunity that you didn't think you deserved, and you may feel tempted to pass it on. Don't.

Friday 4 February

The decision to get out of a failing friendship has already been made; it's just propriety that keeps you in limbo. In work, while your objective is to do the best you can with what you've got, others may think it more worthwhile to achieve the minimum needed to keep themselves on track. Unless you stop expecting so much from others, you risk creating tensions that could damage your relationships with colleagues.

Saturday 5 February

Blind optimism may see you come unstuck in your business partnership. Keep it in perspective. Avoid making unrealistic and impractical demands on yourself, as the consequences will be unpredictable. Not a good day for making decisions, especially in the later part of the afternoon. Try to exercise restraint as your energy levels may have you jumping off walls. A general restlessness will mar your decision-making ability and could result in an accident.

Sunday 6 February

Even though you are happy where you are, you'll jump at the chance to explore the unknown, so don't let your

YOUR DAILY GUIDE

confidence get you into trouble! Keep a healthy respect for work rather than deciding you're up to any challenge that comes along. A few days from now you'll be in a better position to plan both your work and your social life, so a nice balance can be struck between the two.

Monday 7 February

If you think you've missed an opportunity to get ahead in your career, keep your chin up. Sometimes the act of trying your guts out is the most impressive action of all. Most energies are quite productive in your family this week, and members are given to expressing themselves with care and honesty. Don't hide your feelings because of insignificant personal issues.

Tuesday 8 February

Until mid-March you receive a boost of energy in your romance and fun sector that will ensure a good time. The appearance of a new Moon means an opportunity to embark on a new adventure. Think carefully about what you want to achieve in the long-term. Decide where you should put your energies this lunar month and sketch out a plan of attack.

Wednesday 9 February

Try to think before making any move that involves spending money, as certain offers made to you will be dubious. Your unpredictability will leave those around you feeling confused and uncertain. Sit back and observe those around you. Remind others that there are no secrets to success and not to waste your time looking for them. Success is the result of perfection, hard work, learning from failure, loyalty to those for whom you work and persistence.

Thursday 10 February

Usually the opinions we form about others over a long time are justified by experience, but in this case you are a victim of circumstance so don't be afraid to argue your case. If you were worried that someone wasn't taking your opinions into account, you are probably right. Try to be rational and matter-of-fact when making tight calls about a doubtful outcome.

Friday 11 February

You have had a few ideas about how you could improve your quality of life and you are now getting serious about organising it. You could be considered a bit of a wet blanket today when it comes to pleasures or romance, or the trivial but joyful things in life. It is true, you are in a bit of a sombre mood in this area, but this is most likely because you are in a thoughtful and contemplative state about your place in life.

Saturday 12 February

You may find it difficult to deal with people and situations that do not live up to your idealised images. While you are not usually the sensitive one in a relationship, your feelings could very well get hurt by someone who is important to you. Try to stop occupying your time with such lofty aspirations as attaining your rightful place in the universe, as the notion of perfection is a strong factor in your personality.

Sunday 13 February

You will find success through hard work and discipline, especially when it relates to shining through and making your voice heard. You will be able to concentrate all your energy on whatever you're doing, and watch out for a successful person who will point you in the right direction. Focusing on results won't get you as far as focusing on the changes required to achieve the outcomes you desire.

Monday 14 February

As the Sun and Mercury form a conjunction in your work sector today, you can expect to be a little muddle-minded,

YOUR DAILY GUIDE

especially when it comes to dealing with colleagues. It's like trying to read a book in the very bright sunshine. Your thoughts are combusting with too much illumination. Try to waylay any major discussions for tomorrow.

Tuesday 15 February
Venus and Neptune align in the social conscience area of your life today, which means your dreams for an improved world can be better actualised. You will feed off stress today and your appetite for responsibility will be insatiable. Don't overdo it if your motivation is to please, because people rarely offer compliments or recognise good work if they are not assessing the environment in which you are performing.

Wednesday 16 February
It is a time for mental alertness and you will find you are on the ball in every area of your life. Try to get things done and don't lose focus by slipping into an overly social mood. You are in touch with the way you come across in your speech and you will be able to persuade people with your words, so there could be much to gain from your non-personal relationships.

Thursday 17 February
Mercury has moved into your relationships sector for the next couple of weeks, which means you will be thinking a lot about your partner and how you can be a better companion. You have energy to burn and the best place to expend it is at home. There is a lot of unfulfilled desire in your family to be a family and it may be that you are the only planet out of alignment.

Friday 18 February
A small person will have an influence on your day. You may feel that you have had your personal space infringed upon and that you have unreasonable demands being made upon yourself. Don't despair, the time you spend today will be amply repaid in the future by the esteem that

your little friend will hold in you. Your need for fulfilment is valid, but in the absence of an eight-day week, your priorities must reflect the importance of your partner and children or your parents.

Saturday 19 February

The Sun is shining on your long-term relationships sector and you will find you have renewed energy for your partner and loved one. The next month is a great time to spend with your family to re-establish connections and enhance your enjoyment of each other. Make opportunities to do something fun with the ones you love. Any effort spent in this area will be well rewarded.

Sunday 20 February

As Mercury, the planet of communication, comes into alignment with Uranus, the planet of originality, in your relationships sector today, you will find you are wired for interesting solutions to long-standing problems, especially when it comes to your beloved. Although you are back in the swing of things, you may be distracted by thoughts of exotic countries or the heady romantic aspect of your relationship.

Monday 21 February

It's time to come out from your shell and to have social intercourse with stimulating and interesting people. It's good to be a recluse for a short time, but ultimately we are all social creatures and we need the company of others. The spoils of war are yours for the claiming, but it was never your intention to keep them for yourself. A celebration is in order and it's a good time to bring the people around you who have helped shape who you are.

Tuesday 22 February

Over 50% of the emotional impact that you have on another person is non-verbal. In other words, it's not what you say, but it's how you say it. So be aware today of your body language and the messages that you are relaying to those around you. Give yourself to the spontaneity of the moment so that whatever comes out of the day is the best it can be. When you put your feelings on the table, you risk exposure to the limited understanding of others about what is important in your life.

Wednesday 23 February
It's a good day for romance. Light the candles, pick a flower from the garden, cook your lover's favourite meal and enjoy it with a bottle of the finest wine. Alternatively, send an email telling him that you are in love – with him. A good day for an engagement or a wedding. Why are you giving so much of yourself to people who don't matter to you when others miss your company and you miss theirs?

Thursday 24 February
As a full Moon burns bright in the sky it is time to consider whether your lunar goal is making the progress it should be. It is a good day for getting into the nit-picky detail and ironing out the folds. You are on a quest to change the way your family interacts and entertains itself, and it has proven to be an uphill battle. While you are critical of the way some spend their time, have a look to see if you set a better example.

Friday 25 February
If you live in a community or a family, there will always be somebody who does not pull their weight and help with the chores. If you are this person you probably haven't noticed, so have a think and ask yourself if you are doing your bit to make the living space comfortable and pleasant. It may be time to change your ways. Re-evaluate your time on this earth and be ready to disappoint those who expected more from you than they are about to get.

VIRGO · 2005

Saturday 26 February

The pressures of modern living give way to stress that leaves the individual vulnerable and open to illness of the mind body or soul. Don't be overly critical of yourself. Instead be proactive in adjusting the balance in your life and ensuring that all areas of your life are in harmony. There are many things that you can do to make things better for yourself and your loved ones, and most of them are within you.

Sunday 27 February

As Venus moves into Pisces, you will find yourself making more time for fun and games, especially in your relationship. This is a great time to throw off the pressures of adulthood when you are together and enjoy some frivolous and childish fun. You have watched a friend in trouble for some time and, although you feel that it's important to let those in trouble find their own way out if they can, you have to decide it's time to step in.

Monday 28 February

Saturn is having a rough time, so you will find disciplining yourself really tough today, especially when it comes to any humanitarian causes you may have taken on lately. Try not to blow up when an acquaintance rings up out of the blue, appearing to want something. You may have misunderstood the request and it could turn out to be a vital opportunity for you.

Tuesday 1 March

Today should be a very good day for you, so get up early and make the most of it. Good friends, good food and good cheer will all prevail if you allow them to. In your soul you are sure that you harbour the capacity to change for the better, but the pressure of your financial situation is almost too much to bear. You will find yourself running on empty and doing the minimal amount necessary to get through the day.

YOUR DAILY GUIDE

Wednesday 2 March
To be successful adults, children must detach from their parents and develop their own value systems, emotions, beliefs and behaviours. Perhaps you need to examine your systems and discover whether they are really yours or whether they are inherited values from your parents. Take time to examine and evaluate.

Thursday 3 March
The last quarter of the Moon brings new urgency to the task at hand. On this emotionally charged day, this is especially great as the tense lunar aspects mean you are finding everything a little more difficult than you would normally. While your career is humming along at a nice pace, you are still a little unhappy about the impact it has on your life. You sometimes wonder whether it is possible to close your door on work and devote yourself to your children.

Friday 4 March
There are two major influences at work in the heavens today. One is the move of Mercury into your financial sector, meaning you will be thinking about money and how to get it. The other is Venus and Uranus coming together in your relationships. This will give you greater capacity to put yourself across in a unique and attractive manner. Combined, it could mean a good day for getting the money for a joint purchase, like a house.

Saturday 5 March
Today is the day to get out there and take a risk. Make that phone call that you have been putting off, wear that outrageous outfit that has been waiting for an airing, ride a hot air balloon, learn to jet ski. Whatever it is that you fear, overcome it. Your generosity of the past will come back to you when all hope appears lost.

Sunday 6 March
If it doesn't feel right, don't do it. You have a conscience, you have been brought up to respect and know what is

right and what is wrong. Be true to yourself and avoid situations that make you uneasy. Remember what goes around comes around and karma returns. Be the master of your destiny and no one will be able to influence your fate.

Monday 7 March

If you wish to be taken seriously you will need to abstract yourself from that group of losers that you hang out with. Sure you can still be friends, but make the friendship operate on your terms and refuse to take part in the games people play. When you open your mind up to intuition and instinct, you give yourself the ability to do the unexpected and gain more from a situation than anyone thought possible.

Tuesday 8 March

Spoil yourself a little today. Do something just for you. Sometimes it is good to take the time to be introspective and to think about ourselves. Indulge yourself in a little bit of what you fancy. It's your chance to show who is boss on the work front, although you might attract unwanted competition from those who think they can do better.

Wednesday 9 March

Our universe is made up of trillions of particles, each with its own purpose and function. If this is out of balance or disturbed in any way, then chaos reigns. Everybody has their own unique contribution to make and, if allowed, will ensure that the whole operates effectively. You must remember to take a backward position and to allow others to make their contribution for the common good. It is not all about you.

Thursday 10 March

The dawn of a new Moon brings the opportunity to start again. What will be your lunar goal this month? You have an impression of being accepting and allowing people room for their mistakes. But you are guilty of putting too much pressure on someone by trying to guide them towards what you think is their own good.

Friday 11 March
Enjoy your hobbies and your leisure pursuits, but remember that they are just that, and if you allow them to take over your life, it ruins your feng shui and puts your yin where the yang should be. It unbalances your life. Be moderate. Your strong will is exactly what you need to kick-start a major work or personal-interest project.

Saturday 12 March
The workplace hasn't been an altogether happy scene of co-operation and goodwill lately. However, there is a job to do and it is in everybody's best interest to do that job in the best way possible. Lay aside grievances and join the team on an important project. Great satisfaction will be achieved. Ninety-nine per cent of being a good leader is to set the right example.

Sunday 13 March
Human happiness is not located in materialism or circumstance. You must think through the relative value of material possessions and have the self-confidence to accept that more is not necessarily better. You may need to make a decision that will sacrifice the pursuit of money for healthy personal relationships and harmony in your life. Don't assume that you're the only one mad enough to be interested, because you may find a few others carried away by the enthusiasm you bring to your relationships.

Monday 14 March
The atmosphere surrounding your relationships is clear and free of tension. You worry that the lull in recent hostilities cannot be trusted, but the reality is that the goals of you and your partner are well aligned at the present time. Keeping your eye on the future is the only way to stay on

track, and bringing up old disagreements will not be constructive, though you may find it hard to resist the impulse.

Tuesday 15 March
Set your own goals and be resolute in your wish to achieve them. Don't let others distract you from what you know needs to be done. If the goal seems to be too big or too remote, break it down into several smaller and more easily achieved goals, and then set about achieving them, one at a time on the way to the greater goal. Stepping up into another league, even momentarily, will make your peers think twice about crossing you.

Wednesday 16 March
Forget about accumulating material things and concentrate on the important people in your life. Relationships need to be nurtured and are in a constant state of negotiation. However, to negotiate we need at least two parties at the table and if there is only one person talking and no one listening, then the relationship will break down. Stop and listen. Don't fail in your attempt to prove your enduring loyalty.

Thursday 17 March
Your lunar goal should be well under way. Saturn has stalled in your wider social house, which is probably a good thing since it has been a long time going backward. You may have felt like you were going nowhere in this area, and this feeling is unlikely to diminish for at least another week. Don't let the frustration get to you, though. Relief is imminent.

Friday 18 March
It is important that we don't get too comfortable in life and continue to challenge ourselves. This is also imperative in relationships. We can believe that calmness will bring us complete happiness, but it will only really lead us to being unstimulated and bored. Keep this in mind as you evaluate

your relationships. Regardless of the daunting personalities that you'll encounter, you are not above intimidation yourself.

Saturday 19 March
Human beings are pack animals, and even though you may think that you do not need other people, the reality is that you do. Be inclusive, say hello to a neighbour, share a confidence with a colleague, tell a loved one that you think they are great. Remain sensitive to the emotions of others, because you still have to live or work in the same room and the way you make them feel will ultimately affect the atmosphere you breathe.

Sunday 20 March
Mars is moving into your work sector over the next few days, which means added energy to this area of your life. This could be hindered by Mercury going retrograde, which means communications go astray and things get lost in translation. The act of grieving is not just a reflection of a person's emotional state, but a mechanism used by the brain to recover and realign itself with perceived reality.

Monday 21 March
The Sun moves into your financial sector. This month is a good time to tie up any loose ends and get some loans paid off that have been hanging around your neck. This is also a time when you find yourself questioning your long-held beliefs and you may find yourself testing your faith a little. This is an excellent opportunity to renew commitments and refresh stagnant relationships.

Tuesday 22 March
Professionally, things are looking good for you. Be prepared to accept a promotion or an opportunity that is offered to you. Clear your desk and keep up-to-date with your paperwork. If you haven't already posted off your tax return, do it now and get it out of the way. There is no

need to get carried away by dreams of riches, because if you look around, everything you need you already have, although perhaps you're still paying some of it off.

Wednesday 23 March
You are an open vessel for ideas and for finding obscure solutions to difficult problems. So don't close yourself to the idea of being a valuable asset to the team when you would normally take a back seat in proceedings. Try to understand the mechanisms of the open mind because you can access an intuitive state at any time; it's just that for some it is triggered by unusual mental conditions.

Thursday 24 March
Work is important and all consuming at the moment, but it also has the potential to be rewarding if you have confidence in your own ability to contribute to the team constructivly. Use the good will that you have built up around you to get things done today. You will actually enjoy it. Don't underestimate your happiness when others are doing it tough day in and day out, and maybe the devotion of your energy to matters of the heart is where you can achieve the most.

Friday 25 March
Venus is on the march through your financial sector, so don't be surprised if you are attracted to the more well-off types right now. The full Moon has bought a sense of urgency to the completion of your lunar goal. Don't dilly dally, especially as Saturn is coming out of hiding in your social sector tomorrow, freeing you up and giving you the breathing space to achieve what you need to.

Saturday 26 March
Life becomes more complicated the longer we live. As we age, our relationships become more complicated and more varied, the demands on our time more demanding and our decisions more complex. There are more things to

consider, so take the time to be still and to prioritise. Decide what is important and deal with that first. Don't get distracted by what appears to be more pressing, but is just more inviting.

Sunday 27 March
Your involvement in group activities will take on a new level as you slowly gain the confidence to take control and recognise the possible tensions that could be caused by stepping on someone else's toes. Sometimes authority is based only on the time that you've been there, and while you should accept this as one of the weird spin-offs of our primitive social beginnings, don't let it stand in the way of sound judgment.

Monday 28 March
Most people tend to have the best times when the spotlight shines straight on them, so most of us are striving for popularity. However, with popularity comes competition from others. One way to combat this is to make sure you share it around and be wary of becoming greedy. It's hard not to worry what others are thinking about you, but in the end, you will be more admired if you don't.

Tuesday 29 March
There are some powerful energies colliding over the next three days in your financial sector, and the result is quite unpredictable. Clarity could be yours when it comes to lending money, or confusion could reign supreme. Try to keep a level head. You will find a great deal of satisfaction and enjoyment from helping a family member fulfil aspirations of success.

Wednesday 30 March
If you hold back and don't state your true feelings and emotions, you really cannot expect your significant other to be a mind reader. If it's on your mind, say it. Clear the air. The importance of making a decision about your future

will be difficult to recognise, but neglecting the need to face up to your choices may leave you bitterly swallowing what life serves up.

Thursday 31 March
Be careful of what you say. There is really no need to make outrageous statements about things that you don't know anything about. It only gets you into trouble. Your words will come back to eat you. At the least you could look stupid, at the worst that tongue of yours could get you into real trouble. You have a fear of failure that is outweighing your motivation towards success, so look forward to the rewards on offer and you'll soon be making all the right moves.

Friday 1 April
As the Sun and Mercury come together in your finance sector, expect to think about how you can get ahead of debt. It's a long race with few winners, so make sure you are at least up at the front of the pack. It's not worth getting behind, so maintain your stamina for the duration.

Saturday 2 April
As Pluto goes retrograde in your work sector, you could find that the change you were looking for in this area goes on hold. Although you crave a physical break, not to mention a mental one, you will be better served by seeing the job at hand finished in good time. Falling behind schedule won't make life any easier, and isolation from the perceptions of others through your low-key presence will lessen the chance of unexpected help.

Sunday 3 April
You are doing the right thing to hold on to your wits, but you should be cautious not to let your feelings muddy conversations with work colleagues. From time to time, you are quite happy to leave the material world behind and indulge in social environments, but today you prefer

to enjoy your creature comforts even if that means staying out of the public eye.

Monday 4 April
Perhaps you must simply learn to live with the troublesome sensation that you cannot control every factor of your life. You are known for your craving to please, to be harmonious and not make waves. When you're emotionally close to an important person, every side of the story is equally valid. It is best if you can be open to the need to explore parts of life that were previously uninteresting to you.

Tuesday 5 April
As Jupiter duels with the Sun and Mercury in your money sector, you could find that the lucky break you were looking for proves to be even more elusive. You'll have some trouble cooperating in a group setting because your impulse will be to set your own pace. You are out of touch with your feelings as the weight of work drags you down.

Wednesday 6 April
Your ability to talk yourself up in your vocation continues, but you may have foot in mouth disease where all other aspects of your life are concerned. At long last your brain has caught up with your desires, and you are now on the material warpath to nesting. You are living in a political vacuum, which is not such a bad thing, as you cannot handle being out of control. A person you know is getting up your nose.

Thursday 7 April
There is a suggestion of change to the way you think, but some time will pass before you settle down into the transformation. Emotionally you are fragile – you just need to look at a flower and feel weepy. Be wary of those offering what you want as they are unlikely to come through with the goods, or unlikely to be tied down by a agreement.

VIRGO · 2005

Friday 8 April
Decide today where you want to devote your energies over the next lunar month. The new Moon brings a fresh beginning. Your passion for learning is in high gear and so is your ability to soak up the knowledge. Don't be afraid to take on way more than you can reasonably chew, because this will maximise the benefits to be gained over the next few days.

Saturday 9 April
You are feeling right at home when speaking your mind. You are telling it like it is when it comes to talk of self-development or even how to run a family. You will find an ally at home who will take pleasure in your eccentric mood. Remember that belligerence and bellyaching will win you no arguments. Working through such problems will be achieved by very perceptive communication.

Sunday 10 April
Every one of your words is loaded with subtle emotional messages that might have little effect in a work context. You would like to work with others in a way that no one is boss and everyone acts in accord. Unless you are on buddy terms together with someone notable, you will have to simply put your head down and your hand up for greater responsibility.

Monday 11 April
If you have time for the petty needs of others, you have time enough to do a little for yourself. Just make sure that your ideas work in the real world and are not going to drop around your ankles anytime soon. You are radiating good feeling in your place of work and folks have noticed, although you may not achieve any more or less than normal.

Tuesday 12 April
The trouble isn't that you are making mistakes, but that you are not acknowledging them. There are situations that

give you an amazing sense of what is possible, which makes some people begrudge you because they have a very simple concept of high achievement. Good luck is on your side and you can take risks today, but be certain that your bases are covered first.

Wednesday 13 April
Mars and Neptune complete a pas de deux in your work sector today, meaning you will be able to work towards your dreams in an industrious way. You may as well give in and stop trying to maintain your ageing belief system in the face of evidence that debunks it. It's not worth the struggle. Look to consolidate trust between yourself and someone you love as a way to see you through hard times.

Thursday 14 April
You have had a false concept of how to succeed in your job, and disappointments over time have killed off the bogus notions of what a good job should be. Don't be scared to admit that you could do with some time to yourself, as it could come and take you by the horns if you overlook it. Make time for those you genuinely care about.

Friday 15 April
This is a time of regeneration where you fuse the lessons of the past few months and take stock of every area of your life. If you are geared up for a transformation you will love the changes, but if you are pretty happy the way you are then cancel any arrangements to avoid disappointment. Even if this is a workday, make the most of your breaks by taking a stroll.

Saturday 16 April
Venus sits down for a deep and meaningful in your education sector and you will find reading and schooling more attractive. An overseas trip sounds pretty good right now, and if you are planning to travel over the coming weeks, you are sure to find yourself in more than one art gallery

or beautiful building. If renovating, you may have the impulse to decorate with objects from different cultures. An exotic bird could capture your heart.

Sunday 17 April
Your otherwise good relationships in the home and family have become tense. Do something special to set your mind on a different path, and see what you come up with. You are very much regarded among your peers for your readiness to lend a hand to those in need, so try not to let petty differences stand in the way of your otherwise valiant efforts.

Monday 18 April
If you have a short-term ambition in your sights and have set off to achieve it, swallow your fear of failure because you are guaranteed victory. You may be able to get out of your economic rut by taking on a second job, but things won't get that bad if you plan well. You possess the sort of energy levels that help you carry on through fatigue.

Tuesday 19 April
You usually call on instinct when under pressure, but for one reason or another this option is not open to you this time. You may need to glance again at your career choice and see if you haven't taken the wrong turn. You may not be entirely aware of your own impetus in your dealings with close friends.

Wednesday 20 April
The Sun is highlighting the big picture for you. This month is a great time to assess the progress of your long-term goals. Are you where you want to be? Think about your priorities. Have they changed and do you need to alter your life goals accordingly? Sometimes we can doggedly follow a dream even when that dream no longer sparkles for us. This month is also great for planning a long trip.

YOUR DAILY GUIDE

Thursday 21 April
Your brain, emotions and ego are in harmony today and you will be able to make large material gains if you so desire. Look for physical outlets for your energy, especially in team sports with constant action. Try to divert your mind if your body is limited to one place or you will feel a bit like a splodge without any focus or arena for action.

Friday 22 April
It is easy to feel at fault if your finances aren't in order, but maybe it's because you haven't set any realistic financial goals; instead you prefer to put your money anywhere your mouth is. Be kind to all you know these days, because you are liable to break out in little spasms of resentment and they may glimpse a hot-blooded side to you that they didn't know existed.

Saturday 23 April
You might not realise it yet, but over the last couple of days you have met somebody who may be a very fruitful business partner, or may well turn into something a little more hot and heavy. It's a magnificent time to be alive, so why are you waiting to act when you know what to do? If you didn't jump into a new situation yesterday, then today you certainly must.

Sunday 24 April
The pregnant Moon wends its way across the sky tonight, signalling the zenith of your lunar energy. If you are feeling financial strain, you'll be sacrificing a lot more at the moment and it will be worth your while to develop your knowledge while your material inventory remains in a state of flux. You have no patience with people talking about things they don't have the guts to do and everything they say will sound like excuses to your critical mind.

Monday 25 April
If you want it badly enough, you'll find a way to achieve your highest goals. If anything, seek other people's counsel

for evidence that you are going in the right direction. In due course, you will have to let loose the reins of your ambition or risk burning out, but until then you should enjoy the ride of passion. With luck, you will find an extra bit of cash to get your through the weekend.

Tuesday 26 April
You may find that someone you owe money to will be open to negotiation today as all channels of communication are clear in this area. Your idle remarks will have a distressing effect that you should be well equipped for. You will find yourself under a lot of strain today to perform a task that you never claimed to be an authority of, but just close your eyes and bluff it.

Wednesday 27 April
It is one of those days when even a commercial for nappies has you reaching for the tissues. Be on your best behaviour at a get-together tonight, since a chance meeting won't go well unless you are composed. You are finding your colleagues refreshing because no one speaks of personal issues and you can keep your mind focussed. Those you treat well today might be the people who are there in your time of need.

Thursday 28 April
You will find that blaming your enemies or even your business peers is making you feel better – of course, this feeling won't last. So it might be better to redirect your creative energy into other areas that last and won't hurt your relationships. If you have had kids for a while now, you will have begun to appreciate that total loyalty comes at a cost to your higher values and ambitions.

Friday 29 April
If you have a job in the media or marketing, you might find the approaching days more traumatic as issues get aired, or projects take surprising twists and turns. As much

as possible, work through issues that are playing on your partner's mind, even if you feel your dignity is under challenge. It is best to purge festering grievances.

Saturday 30 April

You are in a charismatic and spirited mood, and you woo with your verbal skill and imaginative expressions. You may protest that you never embellish a story, you just remember big and have every reason to go with your intuition. A modest rebirth is going ahead as the universe intended, so don't resist change or you may not get all you deserve.

Sunday 1 May

Your relationship will get a shot in the arm when Mars enters your relationship sector today. Expect to have more energy for your partner over the coming weeks, especially in physical ways and when it comes to sorting out any issues that have been simmering between you. This is also true of business partners, and you will gain threefold in any investment of energy right now.

Monday 2 May

You have to be confident to take a look at your expenditure so that you can balance it out and spread your money through the various spheres of your life. You will be creative and will have the tenacity to make transformations, tidy up situations and resolve differences with your abundant energy. You will have a pure emotional connection with your companion today, but could cause confusion if taken for granted.

Tuesday 3 May

Try to be a little more open-minded in your thinking about money and play with a few unusual approaches. If you can trust your financial stability, it is a time to take hold of those elusive opportunities that come along only once in a while. You find reassurance in the mundaneness of grunt work and will find yourself relishing the rhythmic tasks over those that need more intellect and input.

Wednesday 4 May
You find consolation in work and will thoroughly relish things you normally only enjoy in small doses. This month will bring many challenges in the area of study and information gathering. Today might be rather busy, so great pleasures like hearing from family can be lost in the turmoil. As soon as you get a chance, you should invite your family for a meal or simply make a few phone calls to catch up.

Thursday 5 May
Keep both eyes wide open and an ear to the ground. Luck is on your side if you can offer a suitable countenance in spite of your emotional state. If you seem to be hitting your head against an emotional glass ceiling, try to unlearn in order to relearn better the second time. Unusual circumstances leave conflicting ideas in your mind and you will be forced to accept that they are all really against your better judgement.

Friday 6 May
You are fuelled by unrelenting energy and acting unconventional in almost every way; you are the undying optimist who doesn't know the meaning of the word no. Today is the day to sit down and write down your ideas. Take priority in your family and your relatives will profit from new insights about issues in many areas that are not accessible to them.

Saturday 7 May
You are all set to go it alone in an important endeavour and you know that you have all the resources you need at your disposal. The concentration that has accompanied your work with other people has been nothing less than draining and you are in no mood to undergo more of this

torture. In looking for constant bustle and stimulation, you may overdo it so remember to review your own condition periodically.

Sunday 8 May

A new Moon offers a chance to try again. Work out your lunar goal for this month and resolve to make a difference. You crave organisation and want to get things established, and you have your 'boss' hat on with the peak to the front. Just make sure you are not being too overbearing or you might find that you get more than you bargained for.

Monday 9 May

Be sympathetic of people who work hard without expecting kudos, because chances are they are overlooked for reward. You may relate to such people if you keep on your current path. A general restlessness will affect your decision-making ability in your home life. Your misgivings are characteristic of being out of place in your own home. Difficult times, but well remunerated if you demand it.

Tuesday 10 May

Venus makes her stylish way into your careers sector and you will find pursuing your ambitions an attractive pursuit right now. An advertisement in the paper may capture your eye and lead to an opportunity to expand your horizons. Make a point of engaging your superiors with some new ideas for the business and you could find that they have a few ambitions for you as well.

Wednesday 11 May

The pressure of being everyone's friend might be getting to you, so stop agreeing to attend every social event that comes up. Take some time out to have a bath or read a book and benefit from your own company. You are offside with someone because of their need to challenge you as the recognised authority on various matters. Try to avoid offering information that isn't solicited.

VIRGO · 2005

Thursday 12 May

You may have been feeling on the outer, because of interests and behaviour that others find difficult to understand. With excellent communication skills, you will be able to explain your situation better today and make more sense. You have made good progress in combining your open mind with a strong willpower in domestic matters, although maybe it's time to roll up your sleeves and get your hands dirty.

Friday 13 May

Your brain moves into top gear today as Mercury parks in your education sector. You are lightning quick, especially when it comes to communicating your established knowledge. A trip overseas sounds like a good idea. Try to keep your eye on the ball, rather than focus on the stitching that encases it.

Saturday 14 May

Your knack to renew your energy by natural means will get a kick along today, and an unexpected event will open up a new realm of thinking about your path. Be dubious of any urge to speculate or bet. This is a good month for establishing a pattern of physical exercise, but don't expect the momentum to carry you more than a couple of weeks – find an exercise buddy.

Sunday 15 May

Fulfilling your deepest dreams and desires is given a helping hand today as Mars and Neptune join forces in your relationships sector today. This is especially true if your desires revolve around the areas of business partnership or romantic partnering. Use this energy well, especially in one-on-one situations.

Monday 16 May

You will encounter someone who is depressed and the most important thing is that you don't overlook their need for contact. You are certainly not one to brag about your life as an illustration of success, rather you know that each life is full of little achievement that lead one step closer to personal fulfilment. Sacrificing a little of your time will have many positive benefits.

Tuesday 17 May

At this time you will bring your talents to the fore in an ambitious way. A good chat with a sister or brother or a good friend is sufficient to get your confidence back up again. You'll need to watch out for bruised egos along the way. This period will see many challenges to your relationships with friends and acquaintances.

Wednesday 18 May

If you have been renovating, building or just refurnishing, you are coming into the first stage of a long period of enjoyment. Mentally, you are full to bursting with noble ideas about how you can change the world and it is your challenge to refine ways to communicate them. You may find yourself put out by someone who is acting in a condescending way. Keep yourself composed in order to react in a dignified and constructive way.

Thursday 19 May

A sense of comfort in your relationship is only matched by the need for independence, concepts that could be at odds with each other. Don't overlook old philosophies and religions for a new perspective on your modern problems. Be ready to go beyond the call of duty today, as situations turn out to be a little frenzied and no one knows precisely how to defuse unexpected tension.

Friday 20 May

There are many resources you can draw upon within your family and home life. This can come in the form of a shoulder to cry on or some help in the garden. Try to think creatively about how to shine in your working life. When you err on the side of caution in your relationships, you inevitably wonder if you are getting the most out of what life offers you.

Saturday 21 May
Your career is highlighted this month. The Sun illuminates your personal ambitions and it is a good time to work towards that promotion or get yourself noticed in the classroom. Don't be shy. It is your time to shine. Put yourself forward for something that would ordinarily make you nervous, such as public speaking, and reap the rewards.

Sunday 22 May
Sometimes you wish you could transform yourself, and this is probably due to recent events that humiliated you. It is not a good day to make speeches and presentations as you may let recent events affect your confidence. You need to be much more resourceful and careful about what you offer humanity. If the rewards don't match the sacrifice, rethink your position.

Monday 23 May
A golden orb fills the sky, with energy radiating like the vibrations from a well-struck cymbal. Assess where you are on your lunar path. It is easy to see some things as out of reach because of the multitude of small steps, but when there are no major hiccups, such projects can be completed in record time. Be careful to acknowledge the support of others.

Tuesday 24 May
You are having trouble reconciling your need for money with the conviction that it doesn't make the world go round. If others appear to be dancing to the tune of the dollar, don't doubt that they have other concurs that they keep veiled below the surface. You seek paternalistic comfort at the moment and this could trigger behaviour that may have to be controlled if no one will put their foot down for you.

YOUR DAILY GUIDE

Wednesday 25 May
While you are finding it hard to maintain a sense of composure under pressure, you will appreciate a friend taking you in and making you feel at home. Don't fear coming under criticism for your efforts, since most people will respect you for putting in the attempt when others would run away in fear. Either way, you have the ability to find peaceful fulfilment in the arms of your mate.

Thursday 26 May
Try not to plan too much work at the moment, because you won't be happy with the results. There will be enough work dealing with subconscious urges that arise out of your recent past. Your desire to travel has kicked back in and you are starting to want to move those itchy feet, but it is almost certainly a good time to stick around and build up your savings.

Friday 27 May
Things are going your way and fortune is on your side. Dedication to any worthy cause will come effortlessly, but you will find yourself distracted by the material realm. An alluring person will lead you and others to feeling the same way on a particular issue. Your competitive temperament will come to the fore today. There will be some sort of monetary reward for your good work.

Saturday 28 May
Your deep longings continue to distract you, and the theme is travel and education. Subtlety is the key to any encounter, but there's always room for upgrading once the ground rules are laid. Just try to keep it in perspective and don't blow issues up any bigger they need to be. Complete all the little projects that have been hanging around.

Sunday 29 May
The temperature is rising in your career over the next few weeks as Mercury boosts your ambitions. This is a time

when your mental energies are all pointing to the destination you have been heading. Hopefully, when you look into distance, your destination is a place where you want to end up. For some, it will be a period of adjustment when they realise they have been trying to achieve something that is no longer important to them.

Monday 30 May
Today is a good time to clear your mind of disorder by removing yourself from material distraction. Friends may be a little obstinate, so be cautious about the games that are being played. Success will depend on the accuracy of your interpretation. You are liable to act impulsively and throw yourself into unusual situations, which is always a positive thing when you are in a funk.

Tuesday 31 May
Sometimes you might get very agitated at work with people who put little effort into their careers and prefer to pass the time with unnecessary on-the-job socialising. It's true, you don't need to be reminded about what others do on the weekend. You've been thinking about your vocation and the level you have reached as a consequence of your hard work.

Wednesday 1 June
It is in your power to respond assertively, if only verbally, and enforce your superiority in your area of expertise. But your candid approach needs a little common sense to make it work. Somehow your vigour is blocked by negative influences that you cannot name, so try to stay noncombative and don't resort to bad-mouthing others as a defensive measure.

Thursday 2 June
You are beginning to wonder just how much some people gossip, as it could soon cause tension for no good reason. Some people want kudos for every little thing, but this is

YOUR DAILY GUIDE

truly irritating when you can see that their attitudes remain divisive. In truth, you are not really in the mood for high-maintenance affairs, so be careful not to upset others.

Friday 3 June

Even the freest of souls wants a mother figure to return to every now and then. The call of security, sustenance and warmth runs to the core of the human experience. A situation could be misjudged and may lead to mistakes and future recriminations – nothing that can't be reversed! Try not to jump to conclusions about those who express their intellect through subtle ideas and whose actions are unpredictable.

Saturday 4 June

There is a collective gasp as Venus enters your social sector. Over the coming weeks, you will find that greater social issues are holding your interest right now, and you will have more energy to right some of the wrongs in the world. You needn't worry about that upcoming public-speaking engagement. Venus will ensure that everything that comes out of your mouth will be pure gold.

Sunday 5 June

You say you don't want to get involved with needy people, so why do offer so much of yourself for such little benefit? It is something to do with pride that drives you to meddle, but when the smoke clears, no one will give you the credit you think you deserve. Step back from the fine points and look at the big picture. You love a challenge, especially the kind that will spice up your relationships.

Monday 6 June

A crisp new Moon unfolds like a freshly minted dollar bill, and it is another opportunity to begin anew. There is a tendency to fear change in the next few weeks as you are increasingly aware of the passing of time and the pressure to relate to the younger generation saps your energy.

VIRGO·2005

Tuesday 7 June
Any projects that were sparked off in yesterday's outbreak of mental activity may be put on hold today. You have to try and put some more thought into your calendar before you wind up frustrating yourself. An older person may look to you for monetary advice, which will be somewhat surprising. There is a bit of a lull in communication among friends that will give you time for personal review.

Wednesday 8 June
The benevolent presence of Jupiter has been moving backwards through your money and material goods sector, making what should have been a carefree walk an absolute slog. This backwards motion has been reversed today and you will find life in this area much easier.

Thursday 9 June
The heavenly aspects today cast a bizarre pall over communications, so maybe talking over your ideas will give you a heads up about potential misunderstandings. There is strength in your family's relationships, so try to remain above the power trips associated with discrediting other people's experiences. You are going to have to swallow your pride and ask questions today, because the information you need is only available from others.

Friday 10 June
Your personality has the quality of butter and honey and few are not interested in you. Quite honestly, you could read aloud an instruction manual and your admirers would swoon with delight. Most people understand that you're not a hero, but don't fail to remember why you are where you are and demand acknowledgment when the time is right. Try harder to be a conscientious partner in romance or business.

Saturday 11 June
You will receive the gift of wisdom and assistance from someone who is normally standoffish. Making this difficult

connection will give you an opportunity to open your mind as you relate new concepts and ways of life. You can see the road ahead and will make the correct choices as the mental fog of the last day or two clears and your lightning-quick mind is rebooted.

Sunday 12 June
Mars busts into your financial sector today, giving you the energy you need to get your bank balance back on track. Resolve to pay any growing debts over the coming weeks and get your credit card back to home-base again. This is a very energetic position for physical lovemaking and you can expect to have your mojo back in the bedroom. Mars gives you a sustained and potent energy in this area.

Monday 13 June
Mercury whizzes into your social sector with a whir and a buzz and you can expect your mental energy to be heightened at this time, especially when it comes to larger social issues and dealing with big groups of people. People working in welfare, science or technology will be at their greatest mental advantage over the coming weeks. Eccentric or unusual solutions to an old problem may present themselves.

Tuesday 14 June
There is a duel in the sky between the Sun and Pluto tonight, which could mean one of two things – all or nothing. For some there will be a great change for the ego regarding career and ambitions; for most, there will be nothing at all. You can keep developing with an open mind.

Wednesday 15 June
You are well situated to confront any problem thrown at you by your family or parents. However, as you're very inquisitive, other people may begin to feel a little cowed by your never-ending questions. Try not to ask such casually

sounding questions about very private issues. In love, try to be a responsible partner and deal with the problems you are facing before they fester.

Thursday 16 June
After a long couple of days, spoil yourself with a well-made meal and a moment's tranquillity. Imposing your idealistic ideas about self-improvement on others is a lure you should avoid. Instead, try to apply these ideas while being objective about your approach to them. Strain on your family life is beginning to subside but there is some rebuilding to be done.

Friday 17 June
Madness and immaturity have finally subsided in the office and the environment is such that you may finally be able to get some good work done. Don't fear if you are in a project too deep to back out; you have the knowledge to get through this experience untouched. Everything might hinge on finding the right spin on a proposal, as reason alone is not going to convince anyone.

Saturday 18 June
This time of the month will be a period of hibernation for you, so although many of your little irritations would be better resolved, chances are you can shut them out for some well-deserved relaxation. If you think others are ungrateful for your help in a difficult time, you may be right, but there is no point sulking about it. The trick is to be consistent: reward good behaviour and withhold reward for bad behaviour.

Sunday 19 June
You should be shrewd about whom you decide to take your anger out on today, because chances are everyone has a good reason for their behaviour. Giving some the benefit of the doubt while others do the hard work will only result in bad blood among friends. Craving independence and

autonomy is all very well, but when it comes to home-cooked meals you love to be spoilt by a motherly figure.

Monday 20 June
You might feel as though you are moving backwards in some respect and this unexpectedly gives you a real urge to get going. You will begin the 101 things that you have not felt like initiating lately, largely because you have required a time of peace and quiet. It is going to be a big week, so look for support from your family to help things flow smoothly at home.

Tuesday 21 June
You are cashed up, and while part of you is thankful to be out of financial hot water, a different part of you is dying to satisfy the urges that have been starved for so long. You are in the relationship wars and all you can do is keep your chin up and march on. You should try to take sanctuary in your partner but that will seem a little hollow, for your sense of home feels threatened.

Wednesday 22 June
As the low red Moon reaches capacity in the sky, take a moment to work out what needs to be done to reach your lunar goal. The Sun has moved into your social con-science, which means you are shining in your outer social sphere this month. Your ability to communicate to a wide audience is heightened. Hitting upon unusual solutions to old problems is now accessible to you.

Thursday 23 June
You feel you've taken a beating in your work life, so breaking out of the old routine will be a sure-fire way to reignite the old flame. Too often you can go unnoticed if you are the only one holding the fort when things get really busy. But hey, if a tree falls in a forest . . . You are in a think first and ask later mode, which maybe isn't a good thing for your current tactless disposition.

VIRGO · 2005

Friday 24 June
It is fine to act passionately towards your goals, and you will delight at the inventive ways you find to make something out of nothing. If you chickened out at the very last minute of a recent trial, you will have your chance once more, but today is not the day. Stay away from psychic attack if you recognise it for what it is. Remain faithful to what is good.

Saturday 25 June
You are on the verge of a great new beginning, of purification by fire (not literally, of course, but astrologically). Your rather suspicious mood has lifted and you are now able to take pleasure in your sweetened communication skills for wooing the opposite sex. Don't hesitate to say things that you think will cause conflict, because it is this sort of direct statement that will open the door to their mind.

Sunday 26 June
You will be able to speak with flair about what impedes you as Mercury, Venus and Saturn collide in your career sector. The answer is not in your future but in your past – you should look at some of the skills you developed when you were younger and pick up the loose threads of life-long interests. The thin wall between what you are thinking and what you are saying is further broken down today.

Monday 27 June
Take some time out to recover from a tough week by indulging in a hobby or engaging in the company of family. Protect against becoming worked up and irritable, especially if you are going beyond your responsibilities. Look to the observations of people who have no stake in the situation to discover the path you ought to take for success in balancing work with play.

YOUR DAILY GUIDE

Tuesday 28 June
Venus and Mercury rise in your subconscious today and will reside there over the coming weeks. Your mental energies may be hidden from you at this time and you will find your communications are not always received as well as you would like. You may even unwittingly reveal a sworn secret or offend someone with a slip of the tongue. Cryptic puzzles and detective games are fun and it is a good time to do some investigative work.

Wednesday 29 June
There will be a challenge regarding your profession, so don't take any opportunity to improve your position lightly. Take some time for yourself later this afternoon, even if that means getting out of the house. An acquaintance may be trying to be good-natured but you can see through the ill-timed jokes if you stop to consider motives – remember that bias is not justified in the name of humour.

Thursday 30 June
Over the last few weeks you have been working hard to make a noteworthy impact at work. You have always been one to choose the dreams of the future rather than wallow in past failures, but you have made a recent mistake that is hard to overlook. Your profession is tugging you away from your relatives, so make the most of special occasions by turning off your mobile phone.

Friday 1 July
Your life serves to reinforce your sense of who you are and how you channel your energy into your goals. If you can cut out the bad feelings between you and your team mates, you will get a lot further even if you think the direction of the group is poor. Dissent is only good when agreed by the masses.

Saturday 2 July
Certain beliefs or values that you hold are not being given due credit from those around you, whom you normally

call friends. Everything isn't only black or white, and there may be more than one real answer to the problem at hand. Unfortunately, some people learn only from their own mistakes, rather than the mistakes of others.

Sunday 3 July
In your quiet moments there is a chance to think big and build your dreams into achievable goals. Analytical thinking will come easily this month and you might find that your brain is ticking through things that you thought were beyond you. Learn to control excessive emotions, which will help keep your intuition in fine form.

Monday 4 July
You are always on the move, and your fast talking could get you through some trouble ahead. You may easily elude others in competitive situations as you are calm and don't appear to be much of a threat. You partner may see you as highly ambitious to the point of being out of touch, but you should hold firm to your direction, which will yield satisfying results.

Tuesday 5 July
You might choose to see a friend who you can sit down with and have a deep conversation. Don't worry, you will see the benefits of the opening of your soul soon. Working together for mutual benefit, as well as having the practical benefits, will ensure that you achieve the highest level with your partner.

Wednesday 6 July
The new Moon reminds us that adventure is worthwhile and it is meaningful to seek more out of life through your achievements. Take this opportunity to think about where you are headed and where you want to be. Make your lunar goal a small step towards your larger ambitions. With this type of planning, you will find your path becomes clearer. This will require careful thought.

YOUR DAILY GUIDE

Thursday 7 July
You have a compelling influence over people in your family right now, but that is not to say that there won't be dissent when your master plan is unveiled. In the end it, will probably come down to a heated argument and mutual agreement. You might have conveniently forgotten all about past examples of this behaviour, but fortunately this is not true for everybody.

Friday 8 July
If you are a little unsettled by situations in your family life, rest assured that you're not the only one. Take an active role where you can if someone you know is failing to find the right path through a difficult time. With many doing fine on their own, you can choose to support one individual with impact.

Saturday 9 July
Your emotional insecurity can make you want to hang onto old possession so you can be reminded of the continuity of material things. Ultimately, such objects can be taken away, so reality demands that you accept change or be changed by it. You may be accused of being too casual in your approach to serious matters, which is something you should avoid.

Sunday 10 July
Disappointing news could make its way into your home. Make sure that your response is measured and you don't take anything out of context. Today, you may be in just the right kind of mood to take the ball and run with it, so look ahead at where exactly you want to be before the moment takes you. You are well and truly able to use your keen perception to deduce the agendas of those around you.

Monday 11 July
Your quick thinking will save you from getting into hot water, but you might not be able to save others who have

been following you like sheep. Work hard to get your body into shape today and the benefits will show immediately. To keep your nose clean you must get yourself into a position beyond reproach or risk being insinuated if there is circumstantial evidence.

Tuesday 12 July
You have a lot of time and devotion to give when it comes to birthdays and anniversaries in the hope that you will be treated similarly. Feelings about people who take your words to heart are running high because no one understands when you are joking. You have a strong self-belief and this is something that you can usually count on.

Wednesday 13 July
You could take unfortunate events a little too seriously today and get yourself into trouble with those who keep the social peace. Keep your fingers crossed, and under no circumstance should you be overconfident for risk of speaking your mind at the wrong time. There are some very insecure people out there and they will often act against you rather than feel under threat.

Thursday 14 July
Change is not what you really desire at the moment, but it is likely to be forced upon you by moving house or changing jobs. Your dreams are a good source of inspiration today, especially if you can adequately interpret them rather than simply describe them. You'll get a taste of the emotional side of a friend or family member.

Friday 15 July
Don't be surprised if you find yourself short of time or money today. Your task is to find excitement and happiness in simple pleasures, like a cup of tea in a quiet moment. Many people are out to get what they can from you, so be ready to question their motives before you follow their instructions to the letter.

YOUR DAILY GUIDE

Saturday 16 July
You might feel you are yelling into the large end of a funnel right now as you are just not being heard, let alone understood. This lack of power may be due to a large work load that is leaving you mentally and physically drained. A love interest will come slowly, carefully and sweetly, and the desire to learn all about your lover makes you an ideal one yourself.

Sunday 17 July
As Saturn leaves Cancer and enters Leo today, you will find some of the problems and hindrances in your social world are no longer an issue. In fact, you will find that your skills are greatly improved in the public arena. It is not all a bed of roses, though. Saturn is poised to enter your subconscious, putting hidden obstacles and tests in your path.

Monday 18 July
You may be inclined to hide beneath your shell to protect yourself from emotional attacks today. You would like nothing better than to get in the car and drive for hours in any direction, but running away only leaves you with problems to fight another day. In time, you will find that effort applied to such difficulties will pay off.

Tuesday 19 July
What was once pleasurable has become rather boring, but this is no reason to think that you have lost an exciting part of your life. You have to accept that your adult life is a different kettle of fish to the excitement of a stolen kiss when you were young. What is done out of love is impossible to reverse.

Wednesday 20 July
An emotional closeness is present in your family relationships that only the tightest of members can enjoy. This is a good day to talk with your siblings about the stressful events of the past to put history into the perspective it

deserves. Your partner will be compassionate to your needs if he fits in with your family.

Thursday 21 July
The fulsome breast of La Luna casts its white glow over the world tonight, gently reminding you to move things a step towards your lunar goal. You know that mediocrity requires aloofness to preserve its dignity. Conversely, to be great, you have to engage people. Don't think you can fool yourself and others by pretending that you don't care if you are nowhere near achieving your aim.

Friday 22 July
As the planetary ball plays on, a quick glance at your dance card has your heart skipping a beat. The lovely Venus has waltzed into your sign and you can expect your life to be filled with her gorgeous qualities. Over the coming weeks, your presence will be more attractive to people and your words and gestures more appealing. The finer things in life become more important and you will be more focussed on material things.

Saturday 23 July
As the Sun moves into Leo, you will find yourself in a more reflective and contemplative mood. In the lead up to your birthday next month, this is a time to consider what the year before has held for you and what you would like to achieve in the year to come. Don't press yourself into attending too many engagements if you don't feel like it. Take things quietly if that is what feels right.

Sunday 24 July
Mercury has gone retrograde in the sector of your subconscious, which means you might find yourself accidentally revealing a few secrets or inadvertently relaying some ill-feelings. This glitch in the system will last for the next three weeks. Communications go awry for all astrological signs at this time, so don't feel singled out. Try your best to comprehend others as well as you can.

YOUR DAILY GUIDE

Monday 25 July
Today you should satisfy your cravings for material things by seeking new technology. If you think you deserve more credit than you're getting in your business, put your money or your time where your mouth is. Sometimes in the rush for success we forget to pause and reflect on the utterly fascinating world around us.

Tuesday 26 July
Satisfaction is there for the taking when it comes to creature comforts, but since no one wants to go hungry, you need to put such things aside for the moment. Your firm control of the family's finances creates a feeling of security, which reflects your role. Try not to destabilise situations by acting flighty, especially if you are actually planning a change.

Wednesday 27 July
A small but significant obstacle is likely to trip you up if you are full in flight on a big project. To avoid such disaster, just slow down a little and you'll have the additional energy to handle these things on the run. You will be ready to take an idea to the next level, which is getting dangerously close to the glass ceiling of your position in the social hierarchy.

Thursday 28 July
Your thirst for knowledge is renewed when Mars enters your education sector today. Over the coming weeks, you will find reserves of energy when it comes to learning about the world you live in. Resolve to increase your intelligence a little more by taking a trip to the library or picking up a newspaper. Exotic people and places will benefit from your zest for learning.

Friday 29 July
You have made some progress in changing your version of reality, but you will find that some effort is required to

maintain it. The risk is that you will slide into a rut of thinking that you stopped many years ago. Luck gives you the confidence to persevere with ambitious goals and you will inspire resentment if you are unable to appreciate your good fortune.

Saturday 30 July
Sometimes it is easy to see that the difficulties we face are cause by those around us, but at other times we are our own worst enemy. Today you will have plenty of energy to expend, so use your time wisely and don't foil your own dreams by acting without thinking. You need to be aware that not everything you are offered is what you need.

Sunday 31 July
Patience will support weakness as impatience will ruin strength, but you will have to strive for action and enthusiasm today as they are not readily in abundance. You feel like you know exactly what you want, and are coming to terms with the fact that you might even have the skills to go out and get it. Get-rich-quick scenes will appeal – resist the temptation.

Monday 1 August
If you are having trouble finding work or dealing with a budget, it may have something to do with your demeanour. Unhappiness could stem from your home or family, but it's more likely something you've created yourself. If anything, you need to learn how to find emotional satisfaction in simple pleasures to put that smile back on your face.

Tuesday 2 August
It is a good time to enjoy what you can give, so you might offer to babysit some friends' children so that you can allow someone a much-needed break. You can't expect everyone to communicate selflessly, so don't expect to get the information you're after without being a little crafty.

YOUR DAILY GUIDE

You are touched by special friends who you can talk with about anything.

Wednesday 3 August
If you've been feeling a little cooped up in your current nine-to-five occupation, you are probably lacking the mental stimulation needed to make your work satisfying. Be careful not to let the realities of your everyday existence stand in the way of your true self. You must create the space to meet your own obligations and be free to imagine and create.

Thursday 4 August
Your thirst for adventure may lead you down a few one-way streets today, so make sure you are acting out of more than curiosity. Having purpose ensures that your energies are focused. Someone you know is giving you lots of ideas that are counter-productive, so either try and communicate your discomfort or make some space for yourself.

Friday 5 August
As the new Moon sets in the sky tonight, set your lunar goal high and don't be afraid of failing. Remember the little reed, bending to the force of the wind, soon stood upright when the storm passed over. Try taking on more than you think you can handle. You might surprise yourself with your strength under fire.

Saturday 6 August
A past experience to do with friends or acquaintances will recur and you may experience irrational concerns due to this forgotten event. Let's hope that you learnt a few lessons the last time you were in this situation, as they will certainly come in handy. You may need to prepare yourself to go to battle with or against someone you love.

VIRGO · 2005

Sunday 7 August
Anything that you want today is yours for the taking but you'll do better if you give rather than receive. Those around you will benefit from your abundant energy. In your relationship, you stand at the beginning of a long, exciting adventure that some will try to deter you from embarking on.

Monday 8 August
You are in no way conservative when it comes to making new plans to travel or to go back to university. It will be with trepidation that you communicate your hopes and fears, as you may accidentally expose some deeper feelings while under emotional pressure. In the end, you will be content to dream and not get anything done.

Tuesday 9 August
There is an important message to be gleaned from an apparently casual comment over coffee. If you do not get it the first time it may not be repeated, so it is worth being vigilant. Look forward to unexpected fortune that comes about through your good deeds of recent days. There is far too much at stake to stay in bed today.

Wednesday 10 August
This is a great day for diplomacy within your family, so if there is anything that you want to get out on the table, do it now. Out of character with their true nature, your family may open up, too. Sometimes an outcome requires an immense struggle due to the balance of power, and it is to the combatants' credit if a truce can be called and no blood spilt.

Thursday 11 August
A positive mood will be permeating through your family life soon and it is likely that a recent quarrel will be easily forgotten. Each member of your group will connect to you on an emotional level that is different each time, so enjoy

YOUR DAILY GUIDE

the uniqueness of the situation and the opportunity to put many pieces of the puzzle together for a big-picture perspective of your relationships.

Friday 12 August
You have plenty of spirit at the moment, and more than one person will want to soak up your radiant personality. Take it as a warning that you must find sure footing to avoid being put off by needy people. You should engage yourself in nonverbal forms of art and culture today, as you are not feeling comfortable with words.

Saturday 13 August
This is a time for reflection and gaining wisdom and understanding about what has recently passed. Celebrate of the things that have been good in your life. When speaking to good friends, watch that you are not stepping on any toes because you will rely on others to help you through the next few weeks.

Sunday 14 August
All progress involves risk because you can't get anything back if you don't invest. Stop waiting for your knight in shining armour to come and save you from your unhappiness. You need to go out and find yourself by actually defining yourself. Create your own legend by being everywhere other than where you are now. It may be hard to rewrite the image you have of yourself, but it all comes down to playing a different record.

Monday 15 August
You are strong of mind at the moment and capable of carrying out the jobs that no one else wants. Be sure to get value for your money for all things. Being very careful with your money and the commitment of your time will see you through an unusual bind, which is aided by a strong and spirited approach to any challenge.

VIRGO · 2005

Tuesday 16 August
By sharing the spotlight with your friends, you are likely to deflect any scrutiny and raise your status. It is possible that you could go overboard with spending this afternoon, so keep a close eye on your budget. Be prepared for things not to go your way, as there is the chance of conflict with those who are looking for a new challenge and may want to take on yours.

Wednesday 17 August
Venus has dropped in for a coffee on her way to the shops and has invited you to tag along. This gracious presence in your money sector will mean an emphasis on materialism over the coming weeks, and you will find shopping and prettying up your environment your main focus. Keep an eye on your purse strings to make sure this frivolous time doesn't send you in over your head financially.

Thursday 18 August
The white noise begins to clear and the lines of communication free up again as Mercury comes out of its backwards motion in your subconscious sector. Perhaps you had trouble conveying complex ideas and were inadvertently saying more than you should. Misunderstandings will now be a thing of the past.

Friday 19 August
As the Moon rises like a silver coin in the sky tonight, check where you are on your lunar path. Are you in the position you should be or have you slipped? Remember that laziness begins in cobwebs and ends in iron chains. Don't allow inertia to take a hold, as it is much harder to build momentum from a standing start than from even the most sluggish pace.

Saturday 20 August
Do not hold onto an untenable situation in an argument to the point that it creates spiritual tension. If you don't watch

out, you'll find yourself right back where you began. A change of focus will not sneak up on you, but you will be surprised at how others react to your new-found perspective on an old issue.

Sunday 21 August
You are in line to gain a lot more today than what is owed to you. Your patience in testing times has served you very well and you should make sure that you realign your mental image to correspond with your demonstrated abilities. This has been a very fruitful time for your subconscious self and you will have developed many good coping skills in stressful moments.

Monday 22 August
You will reap the rewards of your efforts in your relationship by finding a lot more coming your way. Just don't let things get back to a state of imbalance. Make a date with destiny that you know you can keep, rather than trying to build sandcastles out of apples. You occasional doubts about your relationship will serve to distance you from your partner.

Tuesday 23 August
Happy birthday Virgo! The Sun has entered your sign, which means you have a whole month to shine. Your ego is benefiting from the warm rays of the largest celestial body in our galaxy, which means there will be a bigger, brighter, more ebullient you. This self-confidence seeps into all areas of your life, so expect to make a prominent mark on business, relationships, friends and family.

Wednesday 24 August
Time engraves our faces with all the tears we have not shed. You are tongue-tied when it comes to consoling someone close to you for his or her loss. While you may be full of good intentions, this person needs your support. If you are not able to provide the advice they need, it may

be enough that you are there with a strong arm and a good shoulder.

Thursday 25 August
After taking a good hard look at yourself, you may hit on some life-changing realisations. You can then learn to explore the ideas that are important to you and consequently express them in your interpersonal relations. Your brief fling with philosophical exile is all but over, although you still have a feeling that you are not quite in tune with the general public on a few issues.

Friday 26 August
There is either jealousy between friends today, or you have neglected to take other peoples' needs into account when you made a spontaneous decision that affects everybody. Try not to stick your nose in other people's private affairs, as you go too far when you tell them how to run their lives.

Saturday 27 August
Your emotional reasoning may be clouded by abstractions and eccentric thought cycles. Coupled with the fact that you are in a curiously combative state of mind today, beware to curb the sharpness of your tongue. If you can bring your positive attitude to the fore, your more-than-adequate skills will see all tasks completed successfully. Big results require big ambitions, but they also require control of a situation, including your emotions.

Sunday 28 August
There is someone in your life that you have great respect for. Think about why your attention is so captivated by this person. Most likely, it is because they represent a part of your own personality that you would like to develop. The influence of this person will affect many decisions that you need to make in the next day or two.

YOUR DAILY GUIDE

Monday 29 August
You are usually full of ambition and enthusiasm, but you should be aware that you also have a lazy streak and, if given the opportunity, you may take the easy way out. This is especially true when the situation you are involved in offers little fun or glory. Be respectful of other's opinions, especially those from left-field; the same treatment may come back to you sooner rather than later.

Tuesday 30 August
It will be interesting to see how you respond to challenges today, because although you lack the ability to prepare, yourself you are versatile to the extreme. As a business owner, you will be rewarded for the networking you've been doing and your true customer-oriented approach. What you find fun needn't be costly.

Wednesday 31 August
Today you would prefer to absorb ideas in a less-constructive way than usual. Make sure that your mind is not so open to new ideas that you are fooled by the age-old tricks of shysters. Do not start new things right now, rather spend your time tying off a few loose ends around the house or at work.

Thursday 1 September
You are a wonderfully confident communicator today and will put your best foot forward when it comes to getting your point across. You have been searching for a new relationship for some time, but you may have already realised that there is nothing to be done but wait for the universe to provide the moment of fate. Treat yourself to pleasure but be sure to include your partner.

Friday 2 September
Hobbies capture your attention today, but not enough to keep you out of trouble when it comes to a new relationship. Unspeakable joys of the heart are offered to you but

taken away easily. While love is in the air, you are probably in the kitchen. Your keen observations might notice things that people don't want noticed.

Saturday 3 September
A Moon is born in the sky tonight and with it the germ of an idea. Take it on with zest. Remember that adventure is not outside, it is within you. It has been said that there are two kinds of adventurers: those who go truly hoping to find adventure and those who go secretly hoping they won't. Perhaps this time you could truly hope you find it.

Sunday 4 September
As Pluto stops wandering slowly backwards through your home sector, you will find that the rather unreliable and changeable nature of this part of your life settles down. At least, the surprises may still occur, but they are less likely to be unwanted. Take each challenge as it comes.

Monday 5 September
For some time, you have been rethinking and considering a decision regarding a romantic venture. Writing your thoughts in a journal is a great way to help yourself form a clearer picture of the situation and your desires. Confusion will only cloud your judgment with your partner today and you may find yourself yearning for an unrealistic relationship. Time will reveal the correct course of action.

Tuesday 6 September
You are forcing yourself to look at the positive side of every situation, but it will soon start to come naturally. So needless to say there will be good times ahead for you, while those around you complain that they can get no satisfaction from a world that brings them down. Your blind optimism is making some people nervous.

Wednesday 7 September
People may ask if you're OK, because the stress of recent weeks will have left you are little bedraggled and

uninterested in chit chat. This is not a good day to make promises or commit to projects because you have no idea what the future involves. Try to roll with the punches and stay one step ahead of exhaustion.

Thursday 8 September
Money is for spending and you certainly deserve to spend it if you've earnt it, otherwise it may create plenty of stress. Make sure you don't leave yourself short when it comes to putting your hand up for a big project because failure is not tempered by proximity to success. There is tension between your desire to be yourself and change yourself.

Friday 9 September
Look at yourself in the mental mirror to determine whether your development is headed in the right direction. You need to make conscious decisions that you can refer to in case you lose sight of the goal. You are involved with someone who is a perfectionist and the pressure to live up to expectation is wearing you down.

Saturday 10 September
You should always think about how you can please your friends, but sometimes making a bed for your own soul is needed. When affairs of the heart quickly take on a 'me first' quality, they may need reinvigoration. This is a skill that must be learnt. Attending seminars or reading books on this subject will have rewards beyond the obvious or immediate.

Sunday 11 September
The evening is set to be rich and entertaining, especially if socialising with your partner or indulging in love. Think like a person of action and you should be well on your way to getting some of the ominous tasks ahead of you completed. This is a testing day for you and the outcome will depend on your patience under fire.

VIRGO · 2005

Monday 12 September
Venus turns heads as she enters your communications sector, so expect your words and thoughts to be more appealing over the coming weeks. It is a good time for finding love and friendship over the Internet or on the phone. You may even find romance a little closer to home as your close friends are more attractive to you over the coming weeks.

Tuesday 13 September
You are likely to encounter a caring and devoted soul who can easily take the lead in romance, which will be a nice break for you. If you are looking with horror into the bottom of your wallet, you'll wonder how you agreed to spend time with rich friends. You are probably kicking yourself for having such a good time over the weekend.

Wednesday 14 September
You may feel a little gloomy but there is no need, as you are in a phase of rebirth and renewal and the negative feelings of today are going to help your growth tomorrow. If you feel dissatisfied with your current work environment, maybe it is time for some positive changes and maybe you are the person for the job. You need a little excitement, so look to your friends.

Thursday 15 September
You think it is important enough to fight for freedom of choice, but you must be prepared to extend it to everyone, even those who do not agree with your version. It's easy for you to find contentment in the small and unusual pleasures, but others might get bored. Something is going on at work and you haven't worked out the details yet.

Friday 16 September
Although you think you are always giving to others, remember that one day it will be you who appreciates the help paid back in kind. Support from a family member is

much appreciated because they can be trusted to know intimate secrets, since their fate is linked to yours. The efforts that you have put into finance will show signs of a positive outcome.

Saturday 17 September
Each of us can change the world in a small way, even if it feels that you are fighting a losing battle. The net effect of all the acts of like-minded people is significant. You can't help but feel a little on edge at the moment as bitter, money-oriented people state their case for selfishness, but hang in there and influence the world through your actions.

Sunday 18 September
The full glory of the Moon can be seen in the sky tonight and with this plump juicy apple comes the zenith of your lunar goal. Don't let your rest come before your exertion. It is the definition of laziness to rest before you get tired. A Norwegian proverb says that the lazier a man is, the more he plans to do tomorrow. Act today.

Monday 19 September
Take a little time for solitude today because you can drift back into the hustle of everyday life without trouble when your batteries are recharged. Maybe you think whoever is in control of your group is neglecting its needs, or maybe you are just jealous. You have the chance to add some input, but be careful not to wear your heart on your sleeve.

Tuesday 20 September
Your will and your desires are coming into alignment, but to achieve success you have to start judging yourself by realistic standards. Too often you listen to cynical people and you constantly run the risk of failure. You are not one to make great sacrifices in pursuit of money and material possessions, so avoid any compromising positions.

Wednesday 21 September
As Mercury shakes its booty into your material sector, you will find yourself thinking and talking about money and all the joys that a full purse can buy. Make sure that you keep your musings in check and don't talk yourself into a buying frenzy. Your speech is warm and comforting right now, and you will have some lovely ideas for entertaining friends.

Thursday 22 September
You could let the rose-coloured glasses inadvertently block out a good portion of common sense at work and you are liable to mistake your fantasy for reality. It will be in your best interests to allow measured thought to rule the roost today. Don't be afraid to turn to those you respect for their advice; the new insights they provide will prove invaluable.

Friday 23 September
Your material sector is highlighted this month and you will be in a spendthrift mood. Try to keep an eye on those pennies because you could end up dipping a little too far into your well-earned savings. On the plus side, money will seem to come to you more freely this month, and don't be surprised if you come across a small windfall.

Saturday 24 September
It is not a day to make presentations or take new ideas to your peers; you won't be able to put them across in the most pleasing manner. However, it's not that you won't be in a position to offend anyone, you just won't receive the positive reception you think your proposals deserve. Unfortunately, sometimes we are forced to admit that the analytic ability of others has outshone us.

Sunday 25 September
You are excelling in your higher learning and your desire to see the world from the lofty height of success only drives you further along the path of success. Little personal squabbles will be bemusing if not annoying, and you may

find your quibbles with others are something you would like to avoid. Don't allow yourself to be sidetracked in this time of high energy.

Monday 26 September

As you get older you are beginning to see the grey where there was once only black and white. Try to receive criticism as a way to attain personal growth and maturity, rather than as an attack. You are overwhelmed with feelings of sexual attraction that you may mistake for love. There is some danger in this, so look at the emotional maturity of those you are pursuing.

Tuesday 27 September

Romance will generally be good for you as you're appealing on a spiritual level and your aura is very attractive. This will be a productive day for artists.

Wednesday 28 September

There is strength to be found from a friend who will support you through thick and thin. This requires you to share your dreams and allow others to make these dreams their own. Thinking about all that you have achieved is a good way to lose your way, so concentrate while there is still much to lose.

Thursday 29 September

Your ideas of romance could be thwarted by a strong desire to go out on a limb for a cause. If you are not usually the torch bearer for good causes, this personal sacrifice will strike you as particularly strange. In the past you may have felt like the world was against you at times, but at the moment you feel like you want to embrace humankind with a big old bear hug.

Friday 30 September

You must reconcile yourself to the fact that long-established patterns of behaviour cannot be changed instantly just because you want them to be. However, your constant determination to better yourself will guarantee success in the end, though self-improvement is a road without an end. In the meantime, come up with some fun ideas for spending time with family and close friends.

Saturday 1 October
You are not the party animal that others would like you to be right now, but don't think for a minute that this is an issue that demands your consideration. Be aware of your tendency to follow the lead of others in fashion and whether you like being a sheep or would like to get off that well-trodden path one day.

Sunday 2 October
If you are returning to a job that has been left hanging, you will find parts of the situation rusty and in need of oil. Try to make sure you are not swept up in anything dramatic – dramatic people in particular. You don't feel you have a part to play in an emotional event, but your support would be missed.

Monday 3 October
Hope is on the horizon as the new Moon climbs to heady heights. Remember that you can't cross the sea merely by standing and staring at the water. Even Moses had to walk. Don't indulge in vain wishes and stand by your decision to act, in whatever capacity and whichever way you care to. Right now, it doesn't matter what you decide to do, as long as you do something.

Tuesday 4 October
As Mars goes retrograde in your education sector, you will find that your energy is lowered in this part of your life. You could even become angry or frustrated about your academic work or when trying to get your knowledge across to other people. Try to stay calm and muster up your patience to get the job done.

YOUR DAILY GUIDE

Wednesday 5 October
Your heart and soul are doing it easy today, everything is just light and breezy, and you may be inspired to make a big romantic gesture to someone near and dear. This gesture will be well received. The joy that you bring to the people around you with your flair and enthusiasm will be returned when you are in need. Share your highs with others and they will do the same.

Thursday 6 October
Try as hard as you might to impress the people you work with, they will never be comfortable with your eccentric views and flamboyant attitudes. You must consider whether you are happy with this, and is it affecting your work environment and opportunities? Indulging your own behaviour is tempting but you know deep down that a balanced approach is a better way to supplement your lifestyle.

Friday 7 October
You carry yourself awkwardly at the moment because you are uncomfortable with yourself. Although you desire to stay out of the spotlight, you will fail miserably unless you can work out how to turn your brain off and simply exist for a while. Your ability to handle social interaction will see you through this period of self-consciousness.

Saturday 8 October
Your home is about to benefit from the beatific presence of Venus as she enters your family and domestic sector. This signals a loving time over the coming weeks when you will crave the presence of the familiar. A great time to get some small renovations done around the house, your aesthetic sensibilities will be heightened when it comes to your immediate surroundings. A family friend could knock on the door with an offer of romance.

Sunday 9 October
The static across the wires clears as Mercury enters your communications sector and you can expect to be heard,

loud and clear. Your thoughts are very accessible to you right now. You can use this energy to your advantage in many areas of your life, including your work, career, relationships and romances, so make sure you figure out what needs to be said and say it.

Monday 10 October
A sense of the extraordinary is in your life at the moment. This is a valuable gift to have and it is one that you hold quite dear. You also find it important to be able to recognise the extraordinary in the most ordinary of things, including human behaviour. While it is everywhere, you never cease to be amazed by it.

Tuesday 11 October
Getting through the day will be a little tough, and maybe it would be better if you didn't get out of bed. There will be ample opportunity to show your talent in the coming days but this is not something to rush. If things aren't going your way, accept the flow of the tide rather than wearing yourself out before the real action begins.

Wednesday 12 October
You will be approaching most situations today from an emotional viewpoint. Communications are especially from the heart and not the head, and you are likely to make a promise that you can't and probably shouldn't keep. If your beloved gets a little too big for their boots during the middle of the day, set them straight before the situation gets out of control.

Thursday 13 October
Your mind will be intensely focussed on communicating to a mix of audiences. Today will provide the chance to catch up with old friends, or friends with whom you are becoming slowly more distant. This creeping distance is not a product of a lessening friendship; rather it is due to the pressures of the lives that you lead.

YOUR DAILY GUIDE

Friday 14 October
As you like to be on the move, you often leave behind half-completed tasks. You can also find yourself over committing and getting in too deep. Try to remain centred on the tasks at hand and allow the full reach of an issue to wash over you. If you are frustrated by your own efforts, don't resort to bad-mouthing colleagues behind their backs.

Saturday 15 October
Tensions between others are frustrating because they impact on your work. It may be difficult to sort this problem out because the participants do not trust your feel for the issue. You can get over this little dip in your self-esteem by applying good health practices. Working up a sweat is the best way to cure self-consciousness.

Sunday 16 October
You are flushed with success, but not sure whether to rest on your laurels just yet. Give it a few days to see if you have really reached your goals, or if success is putting things a little out of perspective. There is nothing to do but stop a relationship with a work contact, even though this may be disappointing.

Monday 17 October
The Moon is plump and full in the sky reminding you to work on your lunar goal. Remember, it is useless doing everything efficiently if it doesn't need to be done at all, so consolidate your activities and do only what it essential. At any rate, leave the tasks that can remain until the end, no matter how enjoyable. This month, it is definitely a case of eating your vegies first.

Tuesday 18 October
You are inspired by the most unusual things at the moment and occasionally this gets you thinking more deeply about your life. Be true to your friends as they will be there for

you in your time of need. Productivity is linked with your state of happiness and how interested you are in the matter at hand, so don't be surprised if you can't excel at monotonous tasks.

Wednesday 19 October
Try to think carefully before you make any big decisions. Tolerance is easy when we concentrate on our similarities rather than dwell on our differences. Take heed of past lessons concerning sensitive subjects as you are bound to make the same mistakes if you don't acknowledge your role in the process. The impact of friends on your home life may cause tension in your family that is difficult to resolve.

Thursday 20 October
A secret held close to your family's chest may be forced out and will subsequently be an uncomfortable time. The way you deal with touchy issues will either define you or break you, so the situation is truly a call to arms. Ultimately, you are not interested in spreading news about other people because your powerful ego makes you lack real interest in their affairs.

Friday 21 October
If there is a project you are closely involved in, follow your instincts today and be clear about which direction you believe proceedings should take. Your opinion will be met with the respect that it deserves and may prove quite influential. Otherwise, set a new direction for yourself. If you have the day off, it would be well employed with a bout of spring-cleaning.

Saturday 22 October
This is an opportunity for you to cut through the psychic debris that distorts your ability to see situations clearly. Rather than viewing situations as how you would like them to be, begin to accept them as they are. This is especially true when it comes to trying to get things moving in your

family life. Listening to another family member's perspective will widen your understanding.

Sunday 23 October
This is a great day for communication and you will have no trouble getting your point of view across, even in situations involving groups of people. There is a lot happening around you at the moment, which will require a great investment of energy. You could be forgiven for thinking that everything is well in your circle of friends, but there may be issues that you are blind to.

Monday 24 October
The Sun has entered your communications sector this month, so it's a good time to re-establish contacts with friends and acquaintances that you have let slip. It is also a good period for enjoying short trips. Plan to do some sightseeing close to home. Think of some of the tourist attractions in your area. How many have you visited? This is a great time to explore your corner of the earth.

Tuesday 25 October
The next few days will be a reflective time when your subconscious will take stock of its dreams and limitations and the new goals you have set. You have to fulfil your commitments and obligations before you can hope to move on to new things. Tasks left undone will taunt you through unusual synchronistic events. Dedication is often unromantic but always necessary.

Wednesday 26 October
You have a great ability to think very deeply about your subconscious and the way your mind works, but very few people have the courage to back the kind of conjecture this type of thinking encourages. No wonder really, just because something is inspired doesn't mean it avoids the pitfalls of conventional intellectualism. You might need to think through a few ideas before putting them into action.

VIRGO · 2005

Thursday 27 October
There was never a genius who didn't also possess a touch of insanity. Be careful not to invest faith in people on the assumption that they are geniuses when they are really just a little bit mad. Also, your love life is in your own hands, and you will want to have more of a say than you normally do at this time.

Friday 28 October
Sometimes you want to drop out of your life and be anonymous with no responsibilities. But then you think of all the enjoyment you get from your position in society and the power you have to do interesting things. Don't be afraid to exercise your authority to jazz things up if things are getting a little safe in any area of your life.

Saturday 29 October
If someone else ends up making the first move in an important situation, you might forfeit your options if you don't respond directly. You're floating through your tasks and attracting others with your warmth, but are you achieving all that you could be? It's time to begin taking steps towards a better you.

Sunday 30 October
Looking back over the past few weeks you may see an interest developing for certain types of people. Don't feel guilty about this because it doesn't mean you are growing apart from old friends, although that would be OK. Your new way of thinking about the world is more intuitive and creative and leads you to unfamiliar conclusions.

Monday 31 October
The loving warmth of your home sector envelopes Mercury into its folds. Over the next couple of weeks expect to be thinking and talking about all things domestic. This is a great time for negotiating with family members, especially if trouble has been brewing for a while now. Home matters

will take precedence and you'll find great joy spending weekends getting things shipshape.

Tuesday 1 November
You'll find that people seek you out today for advice and guidance. While you love the prestige of being a much-needed counsellor or advisor, try not to let it go to your head too much. There is a chance that a casual romance will develop into something more. This is a good day to make the most of your communicative abilities.

Wednesday 2 November
As the new Moon awakes and reminds us to set our lunar goal, tell yourself that the best way to maintain momentum is to constantly set greater goals, until the momentum can take care of itself. When setting your mark, push it one or two steps higher. The worst you could do is fall one or two steps short.

Thursday 3 November
The approaching weekend will be a good time to take a breather, both from your workload and stressful situations that might be building at work. You have recently been set a difficult task in your job and how you approach it will mean the difference between success and failure. Don't be afraid to consult those with experience to find the best way to tackle the situation.

Friday 4 November
There may be favourable connections for you in faraway lands, but that doesn't mean you don't need to work for success. Ultimately you may be required to go out on a limb and take a risk or two. Don't be afraid to speculate financially when a hunch takes you, as long as you are clear about the outcome if you lose.

Saturday 5 November
Now you have the respect of society, it is time to give something back that is more than just a token gesture to

an idealistic youth. You may feel blocked in your creative expression this evening, or there might be a discrepancy between you and a member of the opposite sex. Family life should be good provided you are willing to listen and show some understanding.

Sunday 6 November
It's party time over the coming weeks as Venus enters your romance sector. This is a fabulous time for finding friendship and possibly even love, as your romantic sensibilities are heightened and you find socialising very attractive. Crafts and hobbies benefit, as do your relations with children. You are in the mood for fun and love, and when you are smiling, the whole world returns your grin.

Monday 7 November
You might be having second thoughts about a new relationship, but you can't deny that your life has gotten a lot more interesting. You are mindful that your last few relationships have been fairly unsatisfactory, so there is definitely something to be learned when things are going right. Don't be concerned if initial efforts take a while to show signs of success.

Tuesday 8 November
One of the biggest issues in your world at the moment is communication. It is hard to keep things in perspective when so many emotions are running around in people's heads. Where possible, make sure the issues are known. It may be possible to develop a formal agenda in a work context, but this is much more difficult in a social setting.

Wednesday 9 November
There is a possibility that a thief may take something from you and you will kick yourself with anger. Being blind to the influence that others have on you cannot always be controlled, as there are certain people who are more charismatic than you are street smart. Don't be surprised

if someone springs a tragedy on you when you bear good news.

Thursday 10 November
It is a good day to open your mind to the possibility of working in unison with someone. You will find that another person's inspiration and drive will spur you on. At the moment, the most unreasonable request appears to be a good idea. Be careful about what you say in the heat of the moment, because you don't want a fragile ego on your hands.

Friday 11 November
You may sense that something is going on around you that you just can't seem to grasp. This challenge will not prove insurmountable. There may be something that is pitching the energy you reserve for your relationship against your ties with family life. You are very good at landing on your feet, though, so instead of resisting change, explore its potential.

Saturday 12 November
It is time learn how to act without advice and instruction, but will you really find the happiness you desire? Your ambivalence towards change reflects a fear of growth and anything new, rather than your satisfaction with the current situation. People, especially your close friends, will pick up on this discomfort. They may wonder if you are hiding something.

Sunday 13 November
You just don't seem to be on the same wavelength with a family member. It is a pity because you need to be wrapped up in the warmth of home and hearth right now. Aggressive behaviour will only make things worse. Resolve to find common ground. At work, a romance may begin for you over the water cooler.

VIRGO · 2005

Monday 14 November
Although you are happy just to live and let live, you'd better understand that it may not be that easy. This is particularly true if other people want to include you in their intrigues. To your mind, there is too much interest in your actions and not enough response to your requests. Probably the best advice is to plan loosely – the less that is fixed, the less that can go wrong.

Tuesday 15 November
Mercury starts its frustrating course backwards through your home sector, and you may feel like all the gains you have made have come to nought. Communications will be very fuzzy in your family sector at this time and you may not be able to get across exactly what you mean to say.

Wednesday 16 November
Take advantage of the bright light of the full Moon to kick along your lunar goal. They say that if you are not going forwards you are going backwards, which is a comfort for those going full pelt. Make sure you are going about things efficiently and not getting caught up in the little details. Now is the time to get the bulk of your work done. The spit and polish can wait until the end.

Thursday 17 November
As the stress of the last few days wears off, your mood has lightened somewhat and you are able to have a few good laughs with close friends. Being forced to socialise with different types of people is quite beneficial to your development. Also, remember to test yourself physically and mentally from time to time, as this is a natural way to maintain a healthy immune system.

Friday 18 November
Everything feels like a real chore at the moment and your mouth seems to be full of cotton wool as you try to make sense to those around you. It is time to reclaim the space

that you technically call home and re-centre yourself. This reclamation could be as simple as a bit of decorating. Other goals won't be as rewarding for your immediate wellbeing.

Saturday 19 November
Listen to other people's opinions, even if only to give them a sense that they are contributing to the quality of your life. Lately you have found friendships developing between yourself and the people you work with that are built on equality rather than attention-seeking or self-serving behaviour.

Sunday 20 November
Exercising may not be high on your list of priorities, but you should devote a little time each day to some activity. Maybe park your car a good distance from work or consider riding your bike to work instead. Make a mental tally of everything you've done for others this week to avoid be overlooked for a reward.

Monday 21 November
The planet of the bizarre and the unexpected, Uranus, is moving forwards again in your relationships sector. You may have felt like your wider social conscience was not in sync with your partner, but this time has come to an end. Interesting solutions to old problems will become available to you.

Tuesday 22 November
The Sun has entered your home sector and will remain there for the next month. You will find this a great time to spend with your family doing cosy stuff. This month is all about renewing your relationship with your children and parents. Keep your weekends free for inexpensive get-togethers. Make an effort to contact extended family, too.

Wednesday 23 November
Now that you have developed a mature approach to relationships, both personal and professional, you are in a position to make great progress. A dream may answer the questions that have bothered you for some time. It makes no difference if the rewards that you seek are found in your work or domestic life, as long as you also endeavour to find a balance between the two.

Thursday 24 November
Saturn, the planet of discipline, has rapped you over the knuckles in the sector of your subconscious, and will frustrate you even more with the obstacles he creates. Some parts of your life will seem to weigh you down like a stone around your neck, but you only get strong neck muscles from exercising them.

Friday 25 November
Success today should be something that comes naturally, but not something you want to share. People who claim to be your friends will take whatever you have to give, so it might be worth holding your cards to your chest. Ideas for the afternoon include artistic endeavours, although don't indulge in too much excitement as you are overwrought with issues on your mind.

Saturday 26 November
You need to remember that no one thinks exactly the same way as anyone else. You can't take the tricks you use on your parents and apply them to your boss, although chances are that your partner is similar enough to one of your parents that you might be able to trick him. A testing period has come to an end for you and you're ready for the next challenge.

Sunday 27 November
It's not a good time to apply a rational approach to every problem because the ones you are likely to face will not

fit into those square holes. Be ready for a dynamic and creative day; those who are dancers or involved elsewhere in the arts will excel and be absorbed in their work.

Monday 28 November
It may not be your fault that your partner feels hard done by, but it is your responsibility to try and make them feel better. Remember, you rely on each other for your emotional wellbeing, and if one of you is off kilter, the other soon will be. You are walking down very well-worn paths and, although you know the destination, you can't help but stick to the track.

Tuesday 29 November
You woke up on the right side of the bed today. You will enjoy the social aspects of your day, and the happiness of others will rub off on you, perpetuating your pleasant mood. If you are involved in an ongoing argument with your family, this is the day to resolve the issue, as you are able to communicate in a respectful but forthright manner.

Wednesday 30 November
An acquaintance may offer you a too-good-to-be-true business deal that promises to end your financial woes and free up lots of time for you. Dream. Discover. But don't sign on the dotted line. You must do your homework. Remember, if a deal sounds too good to be true, it probably is. Don't get swept up in the hoopla, and remain cynical in the face of other people's enthusiasm, at least in the current astrological weather.

Thursday 1 December
As the new Moon gently swings into action, excite yourself with the possibilities of this next lunar adventure. If you invest your heart in everything, you can grasp many adventures within this life. Where and what shall it be? Make your choice happily, because if you don't find anything pleasant, at least you shall find something new.

VIRGO · 2005

Friday 2 December
You are focussing all your desires on something that is out of your control and the outcome won't be anything like you imagine. Realign you goals with realistic expectations through consultation with your friends. You can't really expect to be on top of the world all the time, so ride the troughs of your mood with dignity and patience.

Saturday 3 December
You are not normally one to open up to those you barely know, but in a recent relationship your tune has been changing. While you are feeling very social, reflect on times when you have wanted to retreat into your shell. Someone you know well would appreciate a hand to get back into the swing of life and happiness. Be sure to stay close to your friends at this time because you will need support if a few risks don't turn out for the better. There is love in the air but you're looking in the wrong area. It's time to call it quits on a project that is not going as well as you would like.

Sunday 4 December
It's not the time to take great risks with other people's money, although if you have other people's money to risk, then you can't be doing too badly. However, it is never a very good idea to become involved with other people's money. Take a step back and reconsider your options and responsibilities. Your energies may be better employed finding resolutions to your own financial concerns.

Monday 5 December
Mercury is moving forwards again and communications will become clearer. This frustration was first in your home sector, but lately it has been felt in all areas of your life. Take heart, as of today, you should have no more problems. Well, at least for the next couple of weeks!

Tuesday 6 December
There are people who have been waiting to hear from you for some time now. Even if you are uncomfortable about

your message being completely clear, it may be time to offer a sample. You often find an outlet for your opinions and intuitive though within social activities. If this isn't working for you, retreat to your study and cook up a better plan for tomorrow.

Wednesday 7 December
Your positive attitude brings out the best in everyone you work with and you're proud to be part of a team that works well together despite professional or personal differences. However, group situations are always a work in process. If you can recognise your own faults, others are more likely to accept your opinions about theirs. The ability of the group to work together will benefit from this process.

Thursday 8 December
The pressure of others is on you to take control of a situation, so put your best foot forward even though you feel like putting up the shutters. Your social life has been suffering from a lack of creative attention, and it is not enough to meet your best friend at the local if you want to avoid disinterest.

Friday 9 December
You have been feeling very apathetic lately, especially in your education sector, but that has eased now. Mars is moving freely through this part of your life again, and you can expect his powerful energy to really rev things up. Move on any projects you had in mind, particularly when it involves bettering yourself through books and learning.

Saturday 10 December
You are not quite in the mood for the sensory overload you may encounter today. However, you can't always control the chaos that the world produces. It is a competitive time for you, when you will find a lot of energy to prove yourself and get ahead. In today's chaotic climate, you will be well served to focus on the fundamentals and forget trivialities.

VIRGO · 2005

Sunday 11 December
Getting over a recent hurt in a relationship will seem hard today as you are challenged to reach greater levels of intimacy with a new flame. Learning the difference between having your hand held, and being tied down should be easy after the rope burns heal. The satisfaction of love is heightened by past pain and the effort it takes to get back to those giddy heights.

Monday 12 December
Your relationship with your mate will improve tenfold if you show more understanding of other people's political positions and their motivations for certain actions. Take some time for yourself later this afternoon, even if it means just taking a drive or a walk.

Tuesday 13 December
Edison once said that he never made a single mistake, each time he was 'wrong' he had actually eliminated a possibility and come closer to the answer he was seeking. Today you will need to see problems as an opportunity for a solution and an opportunity to prove yourself, rather than being a stimulus for dramatic change or failure. You now feel that you are following the right path.

Wednesday 14 December
Your run in the romantic stakes is still strong, so take this energy and harness it for the ride. A short journey could bring a surprise. A slip of the tongue has ramifications that will continue, but don't pay it too much attention. You may not have meant to say what you did but you're most relieved it is out in the open now.

Thursday 15 December
When the full Moon peeps over the horizon tonight, expect to have renewed energy for your lunar goal. According to the wisdom of the proverbs, the slug that does not plough after the season, begs during the harvest and has nothing.

YOUR DAILY GUIDE

Make sure you are ploughing right now, so you will not be begging at the end of the lunar month.

Friday 16 December
Venus has put on her sensible shoes and entered your work sector. This means you will find beauty in the nitty-gritty details and will have more patience for getting things done. Take advantage of this mood over the coming weeks by throwing yourself into work and signing off on any unfinished projects. Romance could blossom at work.

Saturday 17 December
It is time to take the bull by the horns in a difficult situation at work. You have been sitting around waiting for things to resolve and doors to open, but unfortunately a lack of progress is reflecting badly on you. Be strong and even threatening, but don't expect to be successful unless you can understand the psychology of your opponent.

Sunday 18 December
The problem for you at the moment is that you are lacking the confidence to ask your boss for more. You would be very lucky indeed if you worked in an environment that fostered quality by rewarding excellence. Chances are that you are having trouble finding time for your own hobbies and interests, so you are loath to support others in the pursuit of theirs.

Monday 19 December
A tincture of the technological and a lashing of the lateral will be the hallmark of your personality today. Most will think your new ideas are just the ticket, but expect others to think you are just plain weird. You may seem a little distant to your loved ones, or you may be overpowering in your cloying desire for affection. You could even swing between both all day!

VIRGO · 2005

Tuesday 20 December
Some people think that to get somewhere in life you have to be ruthless and scrupulous, but you seem to be doing just fine bucking the trend and treating everyone with equality and respect. You may find that some rewards are not yours to claim, but as in most things, what you lose on the swings you gain on the merry-go-round.

Wednesday 21 December
Sometimes you have to throw caution to the wind and take the plunge into unknown territory. It is important to reflect and look back at what you have achieved and gain wisdom from your learnings. You are fun to be around, but as you grow, new interests and needs arise and it is harder to avoid the repercussions for you actions.

Thursday 22 December
The Sun is highlighting your party sector this month and you will find yourself with renewed energy for your hobbies and social life. Make the most of your bright mood by spending time with your children and inviting friends over for a get-together. If you don't have kids, borrow someone else's! Your playful energy will make sure you all have a great time.

Friday 23 December
The office is not a good place to develop a political agenda, so don't be surprised if those around you are acting awkwardly when you get on your soapbox. On the contrary, it is important that the people you deal with understand where you are coming from, and this includes your belief systems. Where possible help the group dynamic by sharing ideas between colleagues.

Saturday 24 December
If you find yourself stuck in the middle of an argument you don't care for, try to take the side that's winning. There are others things for you to worry yourself about and you

YOUR DAILY GUIDE

need to work out when you can spare the time for them. Feelings of frustrating may mark today – sometimes there is no course of action but to sit and wait.

Sunday 25 December
A festive day for most, today is not without some frustrations, as Venus decides it is now time to charge backwards through your work sector into your romance sector. You may not be able to charm your audience as you would like, and you may find that your natural ability to woo your way into what you want is not available to you.

Monday 26 December
You really need to switch off mentally for a few days, but emotionally you are ready to bathe in the delights of love. You won't be in the mood for talking, so get out to a dance venue where the music drowns out any hope of conversation. If you have been flirting with someone, now is the time to try your luck on a date.

Tuesday 27 December
You were born with a helping hand and a sympathetic heart, but sometimes you just want to break someone's fingers and sympathise with the devil. Try to think about your patterns of thinking and how you might reprogram yourself with cognitive affirmations. Don't be afraid to think big, and be positive when your mind is screaming for you to take stock.

Wednesday 28 December
You know better than to get infatuated with someone who is not accepted by the rest of your peer group, although if it turns into something more, your friends will just have to live with it. You're aware of the emotions that lie just beneath the surface of social situations and this is a time you should avoid them.

Thursday 29 December
It appears that the best thing you can do for yourself today is to push away your feelings. Often your emotional reactions to situations can work to the benefit of others and not yourself. A window of freedom is opening, but try not to measure yourself against someone else's idea of what you should be. Many times you've had to fight the urge to follow, and this is a difficult test.

Friday 30 December
You have the potential to be influential at the moment, but not so influential that you smooth every path you are trying to negotiate. Part of your success comes through modesty, and you maintain this by congratulating yourself in private. Although you may feel the urge to discuss a past relationship, don't do it with your new partner as it would be tricky.

Saturday 31 December
The end of the year brings a beginning in the shape of a new Moon. Take some time out from the festivities to reflect on what 2005 has taught you and commit to your next lunar goal accordingly. Allow yourself to enjoy what you have achieved over the past year. You have come a long way, baby!

THE VIRGO SUN SIGN

THE VIRGO CHARACTER
(24 August to 22 September)
'To insist on purity is to baptise instinct, to humanise art, and to deify personality.'

Guillaume Apollinaire (poet),
Virgo sun sign, born 26 August 1880

BASIC CHARACTERISTICS OF THE SIGN
Personal creed – I analyse
Negative/feminine sign
Element – Earth
Energy – Mutable
Psychological type – Perceptive
Glyph – ♍ Represents the female genitalia
Colours – Yellow, green, blue, brown, cream, grey
Body part – Lower back
Gemstones – Peridot, opal, agate, sardonyx
Metal – Mercury
Flowers – Narcissus, vervain and herbs, bright small flowers like the buttercup
Trees – Nut-producing varieties
Food – Root vegetables, such as potatoes and yams

People with a Virgo sun sign are generally:
- Precise
- Skilled communicators
- Devoted
- Observant
- Loving

On the other hand, they can also be:
- Critical
- Jealous
- Distrustful
- So meticulous they lose sight of larger issues

Virgoans love:
- Perfection
- Cleanliness
- Routine
- Stimulating employment
- Conventions and rules

But they can't stand:
- Tardiness
- Vulgarity
- Hypocrisy
- Idleness

SOCIALLY

At a party, Virgo can come across as impenetrable, a cool cavernous fortress with a moat as deep and as wide as the one Scorpio built for himself. Self-assured and steady as a rock, they can sometimes intimidate others with their dry wit and crackling intelligence. A cool piercing Virgo stare will make the most well rehearsed pick-up line stick in the throat of the deliverer. Virgos are not into frippery. They are even less tolerant of the crude or rude, so if you are going to tackle one with a pick-up line, make sure it is vaguely tasteful.

RELATIONSHIPS

'Life is pain and the enjoyment of love is an anaesthetic.'

Cesare Pavese (writer),
Virgo sun sign, born 9 September 1908

When a Virgo falls in love, it is a love not given lightly. As a mutable earth sign, the movement of the Virgo's mind is controlled, filtered through the senses and ultimately grounded. They may allow their mind to wander a little into romance, but they are too practical to embark on anything that is not a relatively safe bet. They can't stand public displays of affection or overt grandstanding. Do not propose to your Virgo by employing a skywriter or buying advertising space on a billboard – you are guaranteed a terse rejection.

But when their heart is captured, all the feelings and passion that Virgo has been keeping under lock and key are lavished upon the loved one. They are devoted, loyal and nurturing, great conversationalists and masterful at tender moments. Virgoans do most things with reserve, but once in love, they will care for you and cherish you with frightening abandon. They will go out of their way to make the union work and will spare no sacrifice in keeping it alive.

This makes them very vulnerable, especially when that cool, analytical approach convinces others that there is only a heart of steel beating away in their chest. Fortunately, Virgo's excellent judgment of character will see them usually falling in love with the right person. They also have high expectations of their loved ones. They adore strength, especially the dignified and quiet kind.

CAREER AND MONEY

'Be wiser than other people, if you can; but do not tell them so.'
Lord Chesterfield (statesman/writer),
Virgo sun sign, born 22 September 1694

Virgo's memory is amazing and they like to file away the most trivial facts. They make great writers and teachers, as they always seem to have the answer for the curliest of questions. They combine mental ingenuity with the ability to produce a clear analysis of the most complicated problems. They also see the shades of grey in any given issue.

They can be a little pernickety about detail and may slow down projects by being too exact. They are unlikely to be leaders, but when they rise to the top they are hard-working bosses who pull their sleeves up and get into it. No three-hour lunches for this lot, they will work as one with the team. Virgoans in leadership positions have to learn to delegate, even if that means letting someone do a job that won't be up to their exacting standards.

Virgoans can see the big picture, but they love to revel in the minutiae. If they are feeling off balance or unconfident, they will often retreat into the detail and let someone else deal with the consequences. The Virgo mind is enormously patient and will pick over at a pace that ensures no mistakes are made. They make excellent subeditors and software writers because they can keep their mind on track for great lengths of time.

This can also make them a little pedantic and loath to make rash decisions, even when deadlines loom perilously. Once occupied with a problem, the Virgo mind refuses to be interrupted until it has reached a considered conclusion.

Your Virgo will surely have a very tidy mind. Virgoans always know where they put everything, and they very rarely lose anything. If they do happen to make a mistake or be a little absent-minded, they will beat themselves up about it. They find comfort in having everything under control in their minds, and can't understand it when their mind appears to betray them.

Virgos are generally careful with their money and usually have a steady stream of it coming in as they are great workers. They are rarely extravagant but appreciate quality, and would rather save up for something fabulous than clutter up the house with a lot of bargains.

They are also prone to 'specialising' in something or other. Virgos can be quite monastic in most parts of their life, buying generic food and spending the bare minimum on clothes, but they will have one area in which money is no object. This might be on their pets or their books, or on their Schtick and Schtone Blatnophone stereo system with whoofer, sub-whoofer and subterranean-whoofer, taking pride of place in its own oak-panelled room for perfect acoustic resonance.

FAMOUS VIRGO SUN SIGNS

24 August 1958 – Steve Guttenberg (actor)
25 August 1918 – Leonard Bernstein (conductor)
25 August 1930 – Sean Connery (actor)
25 August 1954 – Elvis Costello (singer)
25 August 1961 – Billy Ray Cyrus (singer)
25 August 1970 – Claudia Schiffer (supermodel)
26 August 1819 – Prince Albert (British royalty)
26 August 1880 – Guillaume Apollinaire (poet)
27 August 1770 – Georg Hegel (philosopher)
27 August 1908 – Lyndon B Johnson (US president)
27 August 1910 – Mother Teresa (humanitarian)
27 August 1939 – Pee Wee Herman (comedian)
28 August 1965 – Shania Twain (singer)
29 August 1862 – Andrew Fisher (Australian prime minister)
29 August 1915 – Ingrid Bergman (actress)
29 August 1958 – Michael Jackson (singer)
30 August 1972 – Cameron Diaz (actress)
31 August 1945 – Van Morrison (singer)
31 August 1949 – Richard Gere (actor)
1 September 1875 – Edgar Rice Burroughs (writer)
1 September 1939 – Lily Tomlin (comedian)
1 September 1957 – Gloria Estefan (singer)
2 September 1952 – Jimmy Connors (tennis player)
2 September 1964 – Keanu Reeves (actor)
3 September 1965 – Charlie Sheen (actor)
3 September 1969 – Shane Warne (cricketer)
4 September 1530 – Ivan the Terrible (Russian royalty)
5 September 1847 – Jesse James (outlaw)
5 September 1912 – John Cage (composer)
5 September 1940 – Raquel Welch (actress)
5 September 1946 – Freddie Mercury (singer)
7 September 1900 – Taylor Caldwell (writer)
7 September 1936 – Buddy Holly (singer)

VIRGO · 2005

8 September 1925 – Peter Sellers (actor)
8 September 1979 – Pink (singer)
9 September 1908 – Cesare Pavese (writer)
9 September 1911 – John Gorton (Australian prime minister)
9 September 1941 – Otis Redding (musician)
9 September 1951 – Michael Keaton (actor)
9 September 1952 – Angela Cartwright (writer)
9 September 1960 – Hugh Grant (actor)
9 September 1966 – Adam Sandler (actor)
10 September 1929 – Arnold Palmer (golfer)
11 September 1862 – O Henry (writer)
11 September 1885 – DH Lawrence (writer)
11 September 1965 – Moby (musician)
11 September 1967 – Harry Connick Jnr (singer)
12 September 1940 – Linda Gray (actress)
13 September 1916 – Roald Dahl (writer)
13 September 1944 – Jacqueline Bissett (actress)
14 September 1947 – Sam Neill (actor)
15 September 1879 – Joseph Lyons (Australian prime minister)
15 September 1880 – Agatha Christie (writer)
15 September 1922 – Jackie Cooper (actor)
16 September 1638 – Louis XIV (French royalty)
16 September 1924 – Lauren Bacall (actress)
16 September 1956 – David Copperfield (magician)
17 September 1935 – Ken Kesey (writer)
18 September 1876 – James Scullin (Australian prime minister)
18 September 1905 – Greta Garbo (actress)
19 September 1928 – Mickey Mouse (cartoon character)
19 September 1941 – Cass Elliot (singer)
19 September 1948 – Jeremy Irons (actor)
19 September 1949 – Twiggy (model)
20 September 1878 – Upton Sinclair (writer)
20 September 1934 – Sophia Loren (actress)
21 September 1866 – HG Wells (writer)
21 September 1934 – Leonard Cohen (singer)
21 September 1947 – Stephen King (writer)

21 September 1950 – Bill Murray (actor)
21 September 1968 – Ricki Lake (talk show host)
21 September 1972 – Liam Gallagher (musician)
22 September 1694 – Lord Chesterfield (statesman/writer)
22 September 1885 – Ben Chifley (Australian prime minister)
22 September 1957 – Nick Cave (singer)
22 September 1960 – Joan Jett (singer)

SUN SIGN COMPATIBILITY

Have you ever wondered why people get together? Why some people fight like cats and dogs but stay passionately in love until the end of their days, while another couple might seem like the perfect pairing but finally divorce after years of unhappiness? Why some partners are as alike as brother and sister, and others are as different as a fish and a bicycle? What is the glue that sticks people together?

In the 1970s, it was considered a pick-up line if you asked someone, 'What's your sign?' It showed you were trying to get an idea of what that person was *really* like. Of course, no one can tell what you are really like just from your sun sign, but it is a good way of drawing people out to talk about what they think they might be like, which, I think you will agree, is just as instructive!

ARIES/VIRGO

The Aries impulsiveness can be just way too much for Virgo, and Virgo's practical, critical nature could drive Aries to drink. Aries are intrinsically superficial sorts when it comes to planning something. The Aries mind combusts with an idea, draws a quick sketch with a toe in the sand and goes for it, letting the details take care of themselves – or letting them undo the whole project from the seams, whatever. That is the risk he is willing to take.

Virgos are intrinsically pedantic souls who can't do anything until they have carefully thought out the endless permutations of what could go wrong. A casual game of chess with a Virgo – well, there is no such thing. Virgos are meticulous in most everything that they do. They have been put on this earth to pick the holes in the plans. And this will infuriate Aries.

All Aries needs is for someone to say 'That's a great idea darling, go and do it (before something else distracts you)'. Virgos are almost certainly going to say 'That sounds good, but before you pack the boat for South America, have you considered that this is the year for the unstable weather patterns of El Nino?' Gosh darn, what is she trying to do – save your life?

Or point out that you don't know everything? It is probably the former, but Aries will be convinced it is the latter, and there is nothing that irks Aries more than to think that there might be things he does not know yet.

The initial attraction will be wild. Here is Virgo – the cool direct gaze of an intelligent woman who knows what she wants and that is Aries. Here is Aries – exciting and energetic, with a tonne of ideas. Their charms are obvious. But will it last the distance?

If this match is to make it, Aries will have to recognise that Virgo doesn't ego-trip, she just points out the faults so that the project will go more successfully – it really is a great advantage and one that Aries is not capable of by himself. Virgo will have to recognise that sometimes it is OK to make a leap of faith and that not everything has to be quality-tested before use – trying out new ideas is the only way to be a true groundbreaker, and this not something Virgo is capable of by herself.

Being open-minded and learning to grow together will enhance this match, as young Hollywood starlets Reese Witherspoon (Aries) and Ryan Phillippe (Virgo) have found. If these issues can be dealt with, this pairing could be a powerhouse.

The Social Aries

Aries can be a fickle party guest. Don't ever expect them to RSVP. In fact, the only confirmation you'll get is when they give you a call to ask: 'Is it OK if I bring Juan, my

Brazilian drinking partner?' And don't be surprised if after acquiescing, they don't turn up anyway. With an Aries, you just never know.

In anyone else, this arrogant behaviour would be mildly infuriating, but in an Aries, you can't help but be bowled over by their puppy-dog enthusiasm. You can guarantee only one thing with an Aries – if they do turn up, they are not likely to be hanging off your coat-tails, waiting for an introduction. You rarely have to worry if Aries is having a good time. Aries brings the good time with them, they don't need anyone else to make things happen. If the conversation really isn't rocking their world, you might find them climbing the tree in your back yard, or clearing a space in the living room for a karoake competition.

Enticing them to come to your party in the first place is one thing, getting them out the door at the end of the night is another altogether. Aries are competitive about everything they do and that includes partying, so they want to make sure they squeeze out every last drop of fun before leaving. They are not particularly good at reading the moods of other party-goers either, and while everyone else is winding down, finding their coat and thinking about bed, Aries will be the one to find the last bottle of spirits and call everyone together for a limbo drinking competition.

They can be wildly flirty, especially if you seem a little hard-to-get. They are always up for a challenge but let that be a warning. Once they have won their prize, they might not be so interested in sustaining the passion.

They will do and say ridiculous things when tipsy, but they will expect you not to hold it against them. They are not materialistic and not big on predicting consequences, so they will find it difficult to understand your concern about the imported Greek rug they are proposing to have their limbo drinking competition on. And, when the inevitable does happen and black sambuca is trailed like tar across your irreplaceable floor covering, Aries will be charming and apologetic and will consider that the end of the story. Aries don't hold grudges unless they have been badly burnt, so they will be surprised when you maintain your indignation over something they consider pretty minor in the Universal scheme of things.

If you are invited to an Aries party, be mindful that the invitation could be the best thing about the party. Aries are great instigators and are fabulously creative while you have their attention, but by the time it gets to the big day, they may have run out of steam. A limp sausage in a bit of bread and a luke-warm lemonade could be the extent of their planned hospitality. That's not to say you won't have a great time, because the Aries personality has enough va-voom to get any wet squib of a gathering going, just don't go hungry or empty-handed.

How to Woo Your Aries

Fancy à la carte dinners are not the way to impress an Aries, as they usually regard food as more a necessity than a lavish gesture. Indulge his eclectic brain in a myriad of new experiences – take him salsa dancing, for a picnic at the zoo, to a smoky jazz club one night and to a Hare Krishna restaurant the next.

Keep the conversation lively, and engage him with a few witty anecdotes, but mostly let the flow revolve around him. It's usually a fine balance between being interesting and having your own opinions, and feeding his fire-eating ego.

Like a toddler, Aries mostly likes to play side-by-side rather than interacting and cooperating, and he will appreciate you having your own talents and hobbies rather than wanting him to be involved in everything you do.

When things get a little more smoochy, give your Aries a head massage or play with his hair and watch him melt like butter in your hands!

Gifts for Your Aries

Aries don't value possessions that much and can appear to be quite monastic in their preferred environment, so don't go to too much effort or expense. You will only be hurt when you find the expensive ring that you spent a week's wages on lying carelessly next to the plughole in the bathroom. And don't expect her to be too distressed when you tell her where you found it – she'll just be happy that you did!

More bookish Aries will love books on philosophy and ideas. Practical gifts like a Swiss Army pocket knife will be appreciated, as Aries value functionality. Music CDs are a good idea, and don't be too worried that you might not pick her taste; she will enjoy the new experience of something a little offbeat.

TAURUS/VIRGO

Usually love at first sight, Taurus and Virgo would be well advised to take things a little bit slower in the beginning of this earthy love tryst. Taurus could find Virgo's pedantic critiquing of his every move more than a little annoying.

Also, where Taurus likes to wallow in deep emotion, Virgo is normally in control of her emotional output and this could be quite overwhelming. However, the common desire for material wealth and security may well see them through.

Virgo is all about synthesising knowledge for the greater good rather than personal gain, and about the altruistic goal of serving others. The British Prime Minister Tony Blair (Taurus) and his wife, international human rights lawyer Cherie Booth QC (Virgo), have an earthy relationship that allows them to fly high in the world of politics and law while grounded by their four young children.

Taureans are romantics who play with a straight bat. They love to be wined and dined and enjoy a surprise, but they do not think secrets and mystery are particularly romantic like some of the other signs do. Never try to hide something from a Taurus, even if you think that it is a little romantic to do so, because you are more than likely to upset them with your opaque ways. Taureans believe honesty and trust go hand in hand and will become annoyed if you expect them to trust you after you have appeared to be dishonest.

A straight bat does not mean straightlaced. Never assume for a moment that Taurus is as straight as she appears, for she often has interests that border on the eccentric. Collecting snow domes, playing the zither or translating the Bible from the original Hebrew are examples of some Taurus hobbies. You would probably never suspect they had these skills, except for their annoying habit of making gifts of their wares!

This will tickle Virgo's finely tuned sense of the ridiculous and she will enjoy Taurus' little eccentricities.

Taureans are also very loyal. This can sometimes develop into possessiveness, and they should be aware that a life partner is not just a pretty addition to their homewares and manchester collection. A life partner cannot be so easily changed either. This can be a disappointment to the Taurus who, some time in the past, pulled a 'pre-loved' partner out of the bottom of the pile with the intention of sanding her back and polishing her up, but learned this is not so easy. The tenacious Taurus probably kept polishing long after the oak turned out to be nothing more than veneer on chipboard, tried to turn it into shabby chic and eventually gave up.

When they do find Mr or Mrs Right they hold on to that beauty for dear life, sometimes to the point of smothering. However, Taureans make wonderful, sensuous lovers and can turn any shack into a home, so the object of their affection is probably not going to mind a little of the green-eyed monster, as long as it is kept in hand.

As business partners, Taurus' tenacity and Virgo's sharp mind are an unstoppable combination. Intellectual pursuits are usually shared and both are homebodies, so nights on the town will quickly be succeeded by nights on the couch, Virgo wrapped in the warmth of a first-class Taurus cuddle.

The Social Taurus

In general, Taureans can be quite a moderate sort in most areas of their lives. They don't like taking flashy risks and they don't go out of their way to make bolshy conversation. Generally, Taureans like to keep things going at a steady pace, straight down the middle, with few deviations.

That's not entirely true when it comes to drinking and dining. Taureans live for their senses to be stimulated and they are always looking for more delicious ways to feed their soul. So, although the social side to any party might be a plus, it is the sheer indulgence of well-made apertifs and hors d'oevres that will keep your Taurean in seventh heaven. Make sure you have a well-planned menu for your Taurus friend, something that reaches across all tastes. They will be looking for sweet, salty and sour flavours, something a little spicy hot, and something cool and refreshing.

After that, your party will be a cinch, because once a Taurus is sated, they have wonderfully warm personalities that keep the conversation roaring throughout the night. Some Taureans can be a little retiring except in close company, but others are conversation connoisseurs who know how to keep everyone entertained. Taurus prefers to drink at a leisurely pace, but as stated, they are not moderates when it comes to food or anything sensual, so if the booze is top quality, it might get a little messy. There is not a lot you can do about this. Keep their water glass topped up and they will thank you in the morning, but try to quash their quaffing and you could be heading for a confrontation, and no one wants to confront a Bull if they can help it.

That goes for late-night table-thumping stoushes, too. It is a brave person who disagrees with a Taurus, especially after a few vinos. Taureans uphold a veneer of fairness in their everyday lives that may lead you to believe that they are very open-minded and can see the subtle shades of grey in any political carpet. This is probably not the case. Most Taureans hold their views with an iron-fist and the sort of staunch stoicism only seen in unionists and the elderly. Fortunately, most Bulls have to be thoroughly provoked into entering the fray, but there are the odd Bulls that enjoy some discursive gymnastics as a round-up to any fine evening.

Expect any Taurean party to be a wonderfully lavish affair where everything hangs together beautifully. Like Librans, Taureans have a knack for bringing together the simplest of ingredients and making them work in a harmonious manner. The décor will be mellow and easy on the eye, the food exquisite and the beverages mouthwatering, no matter what budget the Taurus is working under.

How to Woo Your Taurus

Spoil your Taurus. No amount of money is too extravagant. Be sure to make some physical contact, touch his arm, look deeply into his eyes when you speak to him, ground him in your adoration. Physically and materially you must devote yourself to the Bull.

The Taurus enjoys good manners, and the female Taurus won't mind if you open the door for her or pull out the chair. Choose a good Italian restaurant for the first date (her favourite dessert is bound to be tiramisu). Do some homework as well, for she'll be impressed if you seem to know your way around a wine list. Feel free to order a good wine, after you know what she is eating, but don't order the dish for her. She is not that old-fashioned, and she always knows exactly what she wants to eat.

Dress nicely, smell good, clean your fingernails and use mouthwash. Flowers are a good idea, but only if you are picking her up from her place and she can arrange them before you go, as she won't gladly carry them around with her.

Gifts for Your Taurus

Anything that is particularly sensual and pretty to look at will be appreciated, especially if it will contribute to his comfort. A soft wool rug in a luxurious colour (make sure it suits the decor), lambskin pillow undercovers or an electric blanket are nice ideas.

Scented body creams and luxury beauty items are also a good idea. Most earth signs love moisturisers and will be obsessive about moisturising one part of their body, be it lips, hands or elbows. Decadent foodstuffs are always a treat. Look for exotic treats, such as pears preserved in creme de menthe, baklava or halva.

Jewellery and lingerie will be genuinely appreciated, but don't think that you can skimp on quality. Your Taurus knows intimately the difference between white gold and platinum, llama and alpaca, cotton and linen, red and black caviar. It's his life's work and he cannot be fooled.

GEMINI/VIRGO

Both Virgo and Gemini are ruled by the planet Mercury and have a mental approach to life, but where Virgo critiques, Gemini ridicules.

Hugh Grant (Virgo) and Elizabeth Hurley (Gemini) were this combination, as are Courtney Cox (Gemini) and David Arquette (Virgo). Cox and Arquette are a great example of how this Mercury-ruled couple can be so different yet somehow fit. Cox worked her way up the hard way. She was the first woman on TV to say the word 'period' (in a Tampax commercial); she was the cover girl of *People's* '50 Most Beautiful People' issue; and she's one of the 'Friends'. Arquette is from a Hollywood acting family, he loves wrestling; he's in a rock band; and he looks like your brother's best mate.

But somehow they fell in love. Their honeymoon included stops at a tennis camp, a beach in the Caribbean and several theme parks where they rode on the roller coasters. Cox shows Virgo how to take life head-on and with energy; Arquette gives Cox his wonderfully Virgo sense of the ridiculous. Virgos have the ability to see the funny side in most things and, although they constantly have an eye for the detail, they relax by being really silly.

Intellectually, these two are on a par. They will enjoy good conversations together, they both enjoy mental clarity, but where Gemini likes to race ahead, Virgo likes to bullet point the details, and Gemini can find Virgo's pernickety approach to learning exasperating.

Gemini is a born flirt and this will stir up the green-eyed monster in Virgo. The famous Gemini Marilyn Monroe once said that 'husbands are chiefly good as lovers when they are betraying their wives'. Not all Geminis are quite so flirtatious, but he does need the independence to chat and make connections with other people.

Virgo has to understand that Gemini's coquetry is simply another form of information gathering. Once trust is established, they will enjoy each other's company immensely. Virgo will appreciate Gemini's quick wit and they will amuse each other with funny stories. This relationship will reap many rewards with hard work and respect.

The Social Gemini

Gemini is most happy when they are socialising. It is their life's work. They make an art out of being at ease in a social situation, mingling and moving around the room, making sure they can extract as much information as they can in the shortest period possible.

The Gemini metabolism is generally too quick to get them in too much trouble with alcohol. That said, they like to have a glass in their hands at all times. If the party is really pumping, you will know because Gemini will still be toting around the same warm glass of flat champagne at the end of the night, because they have been far too busy to stop and drink up. If the party has been a real flop you will know because Gemini will be back at the bar every ten minutes, ordering another strange cocktail, usually with a theme in mind. Geminis get bored rather quickly and they can be a bit like a canary in a mineshaft when it comes to judging your party's success. If Gemini has started ordering drinks beginning with C, then you know the rest are going to start asking for their coats anytime soon.

Flirting is always the issue with Geminis, and even the most married Gemini will have every man in the room thinking they might be in with a chance. It is their eagerness to please that often gets them into trouble, but it is their quick wit that will often get them out of any potentially nasty situation with everyone's egos in tact.

Should they decide to get really sloshed, their natural exuberance and social savvy means that their behaviour doesn't change that much. Be aware that your Gemini drinking partner may be fine one minute and horizontal the next, without appropriate warning.

A Gemini truly disgracing herself is not a regular occurrence, so often the only thing that is broken is a heel from one of Gem's tottering party shoes. (Geminis are usually a little shorter than the norm, but they like to make up for it by being taller in personality and in footwear.) Along the way, however, Gemini may have broken a few hearts.

See, Geminis love to play the room. They have been known to have most members of the opposite sex mentally picturing the children they will one day have together, but over the course of the evening, Gemini will let those individuals down gently so there are no hard feelings. If that evening is cut short by unforseen inebriation, Gem may not have had a chance to complete the flirtational cycle, and there may be some sweet-talking to be done the next day. Worse still, someone may take it upon themselves to take advantage of the situation, so if you do see your Gemini friend looking a little wobbly at the knees, keep a close guard.

How to Woo Your Gemini

You won't find a Gemini on the dance floor or at the buffet; they will be at the bar, with every intention of buying a drink, just as soon as they talk to so-and-so. Geminis love a good chat and they love a sparkling mind even more, so just sidle up and say hello. They are one of the few signs to actually enjoy a good pick-up line, as long as it is funny or clever.

But that is as far as your proactive flirtation should go. When attempting to woo a Gemini, prepare to play woo-ee rather than woo-er. These guys know all the tricks in the book. In fact, they wrote the book, so don't try and beat them at their own game. They will be quite happy to take the lead.

Geminis love to be touched on the hands and arms, and are especially sensitive in these areas. A Gemini woman will enjoy having her hand kissed in greeting, for it allows her to look coquettishly through her eyelashes and also show off her lovely fingers.

Going to see a film with coffee afterwards at a nice café is a good idea for a first date. Geminis will love having a common learning experience like a film to talk about.

Gifts for Your Gemini

Books, music, videos or anything that will quench the Gemini desire for knowledge will be appreciated, as will theatre or concert tickets or an excursion to somewhere fun. Practicality and beauty are not your prime concern. You are looking for something that you can discuss and that will stir the mental juices. You can find the most remarkable things in electronic stores, or stores that sells puzzles and games.

Anything that keeps the hands busy, such as worry beads, will be well used. Geminis can't sit still for a moment and will love something that they can create while watching TV, such as tapestry or modelling clay. They also love to be as contactable as possible and will enjoy the latest mobile phones with all the trimmings, camera, mp3 player, Internet access and global positioning system. Tiny radios and TV wrist watches are also fabulous for Geminis.

Creativity and a sense of fun will impress more than expense and quality brand names, so think about something with a bit of novelty value; if it has a little story to go with it, all the better. They will love telling their friends about the funny gift you gave them.

CANCER/VIRGO

Cancer may have to warm up Virgo a little, but there is fire under the ice. This can turn into a secure, comfortable and affectionate relationship. Comic director Mel Brooks

THE VIRGO SUN SIGN

(Cancer) and his actor wife, Anne Bancroft (Virgo), have this combination.

Cancer's struggle for financial security works perfectly with goal-oriented Virgo. Cancer thrives when there is a rock-steady home base, and Virgo is able to provide that unswerving support. Steady Virgo helps balance variable Cancer and, with the sort of diplomacy known only to these earthy communicators, knows just the right thing to say to stop Cancer tailspinning off into orbit.

Celebrations are very important to the Cancer. If they have been born into a large family, they often choose partners who they think could benefit from being embraced by them. They just want to share the love, and their maternal hearts break when they see someone who could do with a bit of mothering.

Male Cancers are a real catch because they combine their inherent masculinity and the unusually outward show of feminine energy in their sun sign. Cancer is also a water sign, that is, an emotional sign, with cardinal or outputting active energy. This means that Cancers actively seek out places and people to nurture.

In the Cancer male, this manifests itself as an unusually sensitive side seeking to nourish others. Cancer males make patient and attentive fathers and empathetic husbands who love to involve themselves in the business of home-making. They have good taste in most things and are especially well dressed. So well dressed, in fact, that they trust their ironing to no one, not even their adoring partner. They like to woo with their cooking skills and possess more than the average amount of male domestic nous.

Cancer understands Virgo's fussy ways, and gives Virgo the ability to dream. Virgos can get trapped in the details and they need a vision of the bigger picture, which Cancer can provide. Cancers are good ideas people but they can be a bit ragged around the edges. Virgo loves to trim the edges. They can work very well together in business in this way. As a cardinal sign, Cancer will whack together any old thing just for the sake of getting it going; Virgo will fret over tiny details even at the expense of letting the moment pass. Together they can find a happy medium.

Cancer's dependency neatly complements Virgo's need to protect. Cancer's ability to make someone feel loved and needed will push through Virgo's shyness. A gorgeous pair.

The Social Cancer

Parties and clubs are not usually Cancer's social style, although they can put on a good bash if they want to. Dinner parties and intimate pubs are more Cancer's thing, and they are particularly good at making their favourite pub a 'local'. Not for them the industrial clatter of espresso machines and polished concrete. No, they would much prefer the slightly grippy feel of beer-soaked carpet underfoot and the sweet smell of hops and barley fermenting in the ashtrays. Unlike Leo, who goes out of his way to know the name of the barman for sheer kudos value and for the purpose of hauling in favours later, for Cancer, making a homely connection with the person serving the drinks is far more important.

They want their surroundings to be comfortable and they usually prefer their company to fit like a glove as well. Having too many new personalities to deal with at once can unnerve the Crab, so they would prefer to keep new social additions to just one a session. Needless to say, speed dating is not their style.

They are usually great cooks and hospitable hosts who go out of their way to make sure everyone is sated and comfortable. They prefer to overfeed than under, so attend any dinner party armed with an elastic waist as they do not take no for an answer. Their wonderful imagination makes sure that any feast is a visual delight as well.

They are great at organising group outings to the races or on a picnic, and are usually the central point for social life at work. Cancer can be counted on to remember the boss' birthday and pass the hat around for the newborn arrival.

They love a little tipple and are great fun to be with on a big night out. At least, they are for the first half. They tend to hit the wall rather quickly and their impromptu cuddles and whoops of delight can slide into a deep-seated desire to make it home to their own bed or, worse still, beer tears. They are hopeless romantics and can get very 'tired and emotional' if the mood takes them. But that's just it. Cancer is ruled by the moon and its moods, so you may have your Cancer friend pegged as a bit of a wet blanket one night, only to discover the dancing queen within the next.

They are hugely generous and love to ply you with gifts and drinks, and will rarely let you get away with the bill. They are even unhappy with the idea of going dutch. Make sure, however, you never take a Cancer for granted. They make it too easy for you to peg them into a hole and exploit them for all they are worth. They will even seem to enjoy it, but underneath they will be screaming out for you to respect them enough to repay the favour. Cancer will go to any lengths to be loved. That is all they want from life.

How to Woo Your Cancer

Your average Cancer is usually unpretentious in her tastes and can be downright uncomfortable if she thinks she may have to put on any airs and graces, so keep your first date fairly low-key. If you can cook, invite her over to your place and whip up some good tucker, something with strong gutsy tastes and comfort foods, like mash potatoes or dumplings on the side.

Cancers are old-fashioned romantics and will enjoy all the trappings of flowers, chocolates and love poems, and will give you more than your share in return. Make sure your Cancer knows you are enjoying their attentions, because they can become despondent if they think their efforts aren't appreciated.

Cancers can be self-protective, and don't like to leave themselves open to hurt by jumping into bed too soon.

Still, they will want you to meet the family quite soon, and if you know what is good for you, you will go along. Don't fear that visiting her parents is barely a step away from walking down the aisle. The Cancer woman simply wants you to meet her family, just as she wants you to meet her friends and her cat – because they are a living, breathing part of her life that she cherishes. If you are going to get to know her, even in the most perfunctory way, you are going to get to know her family.

And whatever you do, be nice and don't make jokes about them when you are back on mutual ground – she won't find them funny.

Gifts for Your Cancer

Cancer's cupboards are usually overflowing with crockery and homewares, but they will gladly accept more, especially large serving platters, because they love feeding the hoards. Cancers can sometimes have a deep-seated feeling that they are being taken advantage of, or that they are overworked or undervalued. If this is your Cancer, a pampering present like perfume or a voucher for a relaxation massage is a thoughtful idea.

A well-chosen card with some thoughtful words is obligatory for a present for your Cancer. Cancers live and breathe by the saying 'it's the thought that counts', and will be put out if those thoughts are not expressed. This can be a bit presumptuous, because they are experts at expressing their own thoughts and don't know how difficult it can be for other people, but a little imagination can go a long way.

LEO/VIRGO

This is a difficult one to call. Leo will find Virgo's cool approach very sexy and Virgo will love the warmth of Leo, but where it goes from there depends on other parts of your chart (specifically, your placement of Mars and Venus).

Virgo could enjoy playing handmaiden to Leo's successes, revelling in the glamour and theatrics from a safe distance behind his logbooks. Magnanimous Leo will overlook

Virgo's tendency to be critical, while Virgo will take pride in Leo's accomplishments.

However, Virgo is more analytically astute than Leo, who may not appreciate being picked apart by Virgo. Leo may take for granted much of the work and assistance that Virgo provides.

Guy Ritchie (Virgo) and Madonna (Leo) have made a wonderful couple out of this match.

Leos make great mates who are always up for a bit of fun, male and female. It was Leo Edna Ferber who said that 'A woman can look both moral and exciting – if she also looks as if it was quite a struggle.' They are embarrassingly generous, but never turn down a gift, no matter how extravagant, because you will hurt their pride. And they don't blows to their pride lightly.

They usually possess a belly-trembling chuckle that can break into gales of laughter if really tickled. Their sense of humour is fresh and simple with an eye for the ridiculous. They will take mental notes so that they might appropriate the story for their own use later on.

They have an eye for the decadent and will shell out for the most outrageous things, even if it is rent week. A night out at the pub can be an expensive exercise for the magnanimous Lion.

And all Leo wants in return is Virgo's unfettered approval and adoring silence as he tell you another of his usually very funny but sometimes exaggerated stories. Not a bad deal, is it? Virgo thinks – not a bad deal at all . . .

Leo's desire for a gracious life works perfectly with goal-oriented Virgo. Leo needs an audience, and Virgo is able to provide that support. Steady Virgo complements Leo and, with the sort of diplomacy known only to these earthy communicators, knows just the right thing to say to keep Leo happy.

The Social Leo

Leos are most comfortable in the social arena and they know how to play a room to a tee. They are happy to take on the role of entertainer and raconteur if required, keeping spirits up and the conversation interesting. Absurdly generous, they are likely to come back from the bar not only with their round of drinks, but a round of cigars (for smokers and non-smokers alike) and a range of bar snacks. Money is no object when a Leo is entertaining, and their lavish gestures can embarrass some. Don't be embarrassed. Leos show love through indulging their loved-ones with the fruits of their decadence. If you refuse a gift from a Leo, you might find they take it far more personally than you expect.

Leos usually love dancing and show quite a bit of finesse on the dance floor. That is, unless the lubricants have really kicked in, then Leo's larger-than-life dance moves take on an erratic and uncontrolled quality. Limbs that were once thrown about with dramatic flair but always with graceful precision are likely to take on a life of their own. A lurching Leo on the dance floor is a frightening sight indeed. Fortunately, Leos value their self-control above everything, and they rarely lose the plot.

They can be dreadful flirts, but it is only for the thrill of the chase, as they are rarely unfaithful. A single Leo is in their element in a nightclub, as only their large personality can overcome the lights and loud music to shine on through. You will often find your group coming across the odd Leo in a nightclub, engaging you with their witty patter and sparking asides. They are in their element in this situation. There are plenty of new souls to impress and lots of fresh laughs to be had. Sometimes though, they can outstay their welcome, especially if they don't keep their flirtatious nature within reasonable limits, ie, concentrating on one person at a time, and preferably single.

The Leo combination of fixed fire means that they are happy to shine on within themselves. They *are* the main event. They don't need anyone to bounce their light from, although they are always happy to have a straight-man sidekick.

They would rather be out the front than behind the scenes in any situation and love a good opportunity to show off. If they like to sing, they really enjoy a session at a karaoke bar. They are, however, prone to taking themselves a little too seriously and will not take kindly to any jokes or heckles thrown their way, no matter how kindly they are meant. They are good-natured but only up to a point and that point does not include laughing at themselves just because everyone else is. In fact, it is the quickest way to send them into a foul mood.

Leos love the idea of throwing a fantastic party, but they often require the services of someone who is a little more interested in substance over style and has a few clues on how to make things happen. Leo will provide the pizzazz as long as someone else has a handle on the catering. They make attentive hosts who can make a guest feel as if the whole bash has been thrown just for them.

How to Woo Your Leo

If you are planning to woo a Leo, it is prudent to first take out a small loan at a low interest rate. Leos love to pounce quickly and you could find yourself involved in a flurry of theatre and dinner dates snowballing to an early but lavish white wedding.

Make the first date something to remember. Low-key is not in the Leo vocabulary. See a musical, but use whatever influence you have to wrangle backstage passes to meet the actors; go to the tennis, but make sure you watch it from a corporate box. Leos love big dramatic statements and the effort you have gone to will make them feel more special. Don't worry about appearing to be a name-dropper; Leos are the King of the Pride when it comes to big-noting, and they won't bat an eyelid.

Gifts for Your Leo

Leos are extravagant gift givers, so make sure you get in first with a wonderful present. They can't stand cheap and nasty imitations, so always buy the high-quality original, or settle for something else.

Leos love anything that shows them off to their best advantage, so you might consider a voucher for a session of glamour photography. They will love being made up and fussed over, and the resulting photos will take pride of place on their wall. Another idea is to take a favourite photo and have it cropped and blown up and elegantly framed – the bigger the better. Send it with a nice little card telling her to hang it on the wall for her future grandchildren, so they will know what a beautiful young woman she was. She will be tickled pink.

A video camera is an expensive idea that is sure to be a big hit. Your Leo will love directing the action from behind the lens as well as hamming it up in front. Make sure you include a tripod, so he can set it up and film his own commentary.

Gold is always appreciated, and rubies and amber are Leo gemstones. Board games with lots of dramatics and interaction, like Pictionary and Charades, are always a lot of fun. (You might want to let him win the first few games, though.)

VIRGO/VIRGO

If you can aim your drive of perfection at the same target, you will make an unbeatable team. Unfortunately, all Virgos have areas of their life where they like to be absolutely precise and others where they like to be really chilled, and if these areas clash, this couple could find themselves in a disastrous state.

Like many in a same-sign relationship, you may become annoyed with each other about the qualities you dislike in yourself. The constant self-criticism of the Virgo mind means that those areas of dissatisfaction will be many and varied.

Same-sign relationships are always a little trying. You appear to be perfect for one another, but can find yourself irritated by each other's predictability and faults. It is very easy to loathe in others what you dislike in your self.

This can be the major difficulty in same sun-sign partnerships. Your similarities ensure that you are always on the same wavelength. But it can almost be like seeing yourself through other people's eyes. It is a truism to say that you can't stand in others what you see in yourself, especially when you can't admit to it. Little habits and foibles that you never knew you had can come to light, and make you shudder with repulsion.

The other problem (which is in a similar vein) is seeing things in someone else that you have already struggled with and overcome. Surprisingly, having been through the experience doesn't always make you more forgiving of those with the same problem. Sometimes it will actually make you less empathetic.

Traits that are likely to get under your skin are Virgo's desire to criticise without committing themselves to the project. It's like looking in the mirror and that's the trouble. You will either be extraordinarily happy and fulfilled or it will end in disaster – there is no middle ground.

Ex couple Claudia Schiffer and David Copperfield are both Virgos. Try not to be too hard on yourself or each other and you will find many areas of happiness and joy.

The Social Virgo

Some find the assured Virgo posture irresistibly sexy; others find it daunting. Don't be overawed. The too-cool-for-school image is merely a defence. Underneath the elegant posturing, Virgos are warm, funny and not a little bit silly. They enjoy a clever sense of humour and are quick with the one-liners. You might get the impression that Virgo is a bit of a snob, but nothing could be further from the truth. They are not social climbers at all and they would rather die than wear a flashy label. The Virgo is much happier occupying the middle rung of society and she would be mortified to be thought of as a pompous high-flier.

Most of the time, their cool exterior is masking a certain shyness that is fairly easily overcome. Their acute sense of timing and tempered sense of style means they are smoothies on the dance floor, but although it might not be obvious, they are usually waiting anxiously for you to take the lead. Virgos are most at home around a dinner party table where their intelligence and wit can shine through. They are great storytellers and full of interesting information about a wide range of topics that they convey in an easy manner. Their sense of humour can tend towards the self-deprecating and they rarely turn their keen wit on others, although when they do, watch out!

Virgos are purists in every sense and they will approach their tipple in the same way. They will either be staunchly brand loyal or have a particular way that their drink has to be served. The fictional character James Bond had some Virgo tendencies, including his penchant for his martinis to be shaken (not stirred). You will meet Virgos who eschew drinking altogether in preference for keeping their body pure.

Virgos are fantastic at throwing parties. After all, their motto is 'I serve' and they fit comfortably into the role of making sure everything is humming, that drinks are constantly topped up and the conversation is rattling along at one hundred miles an hour. If anything, they could ask for a little more help, as they are usually unwilling to hand over the reins of any project big or small, even passing around a bowl of chips. Virgos are notorious perfectionists and it is not that they don't trust you to do a good job, it's just that they don't trust you to do a good job!

How to Woo Your Virgo

Virgoans will be drawn out by warmth and enjoy a thoughtful compliment, but will be repelled by overt shows of physical affection or gushiness.

Keep your first date simple. See a film or a show with coffee afterwards, because Virgoans can be a little shy but are never lost for words when given something to critique. If the spark is there, you could find yourself talking till dawn, ranging over current affairs, music, politics, religion and the meaning of life.

Don't assume that because your Virgo is the embodiment

of stylish understatement that you will be expected to be the same. Virgoans are often quite attracted to the outlandish or the quirky. Above all, they treasure scrupulous honesty, so be yourself and no one else.

Gifts for Your Virgo

Virgoans have green fingers, so presents such as gardening tools could be a good idea, or a bonsai might put them on the path to a healthy hobby – bonsais require a lot of care and attention and a judicious pruning every now and then, skills that Virgoans excel in.

Their colour preferences are all shades of blue, dark brown and beige. If you are looking for clothes, be sure to err on the generous size rather than mistakenly get them something too tight-fitting. Virgoans don't like revealing any more flesh than is prudent.

They usually like reading nonfiction, so biographies and reference books are good ideas. A magazine subscription is a gift in the same vein. A good filofax or digital notebook is sure to be put to rigorous use. Lavender soap, bath salts or perfume will soothe that Virgo worried mind.

Virgoans are meticulous people and appreciate it if you pay attention to the detail, so make sure the gift is perfectly wrapped, and the card is signed with something personal and fitting.

LIBRA/VIRGO

Libra loves to hear others' thoughts on any subject and they blithely accept different points of view. Virgo is the most critical of thinkers and is intolerant of illogical thinking. Virgo loves talking about politics and religion, whereas Libra lives by the old creed that you never talk about either in polite company.

Generally, Librans are beautiful people with a sense of style and serenity about them. Just about any advertisement about air freshener tries to portray the Libran ideal – beautiful light-filled house, tasteful throw pillows, gorgeous children and sexy Mum, with classical music in the background. Librans look like they have it all, and that is how they want it to be.

But sometimes life isn't smooth, and Libra can look very ruffled in bad weather. If something is weighing down an aspect of his life, he will be pulling hard on the other end of the scales trying to balance this discrepancy.

The Libran symbol of the scales can be misleading. You could be forgiven for thinking Libra is perfectly even-handed and even-tempered. This will probably be your initial impression, but Libra is much more of a meddler than that! Scales are not perfectly weighted each side all of the time, and when they aren't they are in a state of flux. Libra will always try and pull the scales back. If you have an opinion about something, Libra will look at you kindly and tell you in perfectly even tones why you are perfectly wrong.

And then he will tell you in the same even tones why you are, in fact, perfectly correct.

At worst, Virgo views Libra as wishy-washy, and Libra views Virgo as prim and intolerant but, being a learning relationship (as all signs one after the other are, in this case Virgo learning, Libra teaching) your different natures can also complement each other and both can greatly benefit from this partnership.

Two of the most successful celebrity pairings are of this match – actors Jada Pinkett (Virgo) and Will Smith (Libra) and comedians Lenny Henry (Virgo) and Dawn French (Libra). Rock couple Nick Cave (Virgo) and PJ Harvey (Libra) were not so fortunate.

Both Virgo and Libra share a love for serenity and neither likes stand-up arguments, so there are great possibilities for this match.

The Social Libra

Librans make an art form out of being social. Many of their life's goals revolve around meeting and greeting and making the perfect union, and they take this attitude out into the world with them, especially into a party situation. You would think this would make them the perfect hosts. But in fact, a Libran party can be quite a stressful situation for all involved. Like a little kid planning their first ever five-year-old party, Libra can often have far too many of the details already worked out in their mind – who's going to talk to whom, what the weather will be like, the ambience, the music, the food. They can picture it so clearly, they are in danger of being sorely disappointed when things inevitably don't go exactly to plan.

The more important the gathering, the more Libra will fret. A Libran woman planning her wedding is the classic nubile nightmare. Just the seating for the table arrangements will take more than a few weeks. Libra's innate sense of style and grace will mean the selection of the dress and the flowers will come naturally, but beyond that, the Libran woman will drive herself crazy trying to organise the most perfect night of her life. After all, this is when her Libran ideals come together at once – marriage and partnership, friends and family, and beautiful things in a gorgeous setting.

You can allow Libra that on her once-in-a-lifetime special day. But just once, it would be nice if Libra could throw a small relaxed dinner party without all the expectation placed upon it. You might think that that is exactly what you agreed to considering the flippant way Libra dished out the invitation. Just a casual affair, a few friends, come as you are. So you turn up in your comfy gear, bottle of cheapish plonk in hand, ready for a chilled-out evening with close friends.

Don't get too comfortable though, because you will soon be introduced to Libra's friend, complete with meaningful glances and an introduction befitting a speech inducting you into the Hall of Fame. Libra is a shameless matchmaker and can't resist an opportunity to hook people up. There is no such thing as happily single in Libra's world. That surely has to be an oxymoron. For Libra, relationships are the key to happiness of any kind, and seeing as they're so intent on making sure everyone is happy, the least they can do is make sure you have opportunities to get hitched. It is an act of love on their behalf, so accept gracefully and try to make the most of the opportunity to meet someone new.

They are not huge on self-control and can get a little tiddly if left unchecked. Some Librans have been known to calm their pre-party nerves with a few heart-starters only to find themselves a little too refreshed to see the event to its natural conclusion. Some are even lucky to be able to usher the first few guests in, so if you are throwing a party with a Libra, suggest other ways to de-stress if you see your Libra getting wound up about the canapés. Deep breathing, a long shower or even a last-minute trip to the supermarket will make sure Libra is on track for a great evening and short-circuit them from hitting the drinks trolley too early.

How to Woo Your Libra

If you happen to fall under the spell of Libra, don't surrender too quickly. Let them flirt with you for a while. Even if they push towards a relationship, imagine that it's just the scales tipping to compensate for your cooler attitude. Libra has so much fun pursuing relationships that they will love you for dragging out the anticipation.

First dates should be fairly conservative and tasteful. When choosing a restaurant, don't go for anything remotely tacky. When she says dinner and a show, she means that nice little Italian place and *Les Miserables*, not a theme restaurant with an all-you-can-eat buffet.

Don't go anywhere too modern, with concrete floors and clattering coffee machines. Libra is very sensitive to the beauty of her surroundings, and will be much more relaxed with dim lighting and gentle music.

Gifts for Your Libra

Whatever you buy a Libran, make sure you give them the receipt as well so they can take it back. It's not that they don't appreciate your gift, it is just that they have their own sense of style that is hard to pick. Even they find it hard to choose. So she will go back to the store with the pepper grinder you gave her, receipt in hand, spend fifteen minutes looking through all the other pepper grinders, weighing up their pros and cons, and end up leaving the shop with the one you bought in the first place. But she will be satisfied that the right decision has been made.

Libran colours are green and blue. For gardening Librans (they love to be out in the green beauty), a coffee-table gardening book would be appreciated. Self-indulgent luxuries go down well, and a carefully chosen antique will be accepted with great joy.

SCORPIO/VIRGO

Scorpio will stride fearlessly into a challenging situation, whereas Virgo might tread more carefully; Scorpio may laugh at Virgo's timidity, but Virgo just considers her actions more prudent.

Scorpio commits with driving passion. Virgo will make the same level of commitment but it will be filtered through her intellect, filed away neatly, brought out again for closer scrutiny, a few typos fixed and a clean copy printed, and only then will she be nearly ready to commit. And still she will have a few more questions.

Scorpios require a solid security within a relationship, without feeling that they have a doormat as a mate. This is a precarious balance and must be learned by both partners over time, but it is something that Virgo, as the server, should have no trouble with. The Virgo temperament has the right amount of resilience and commitment to reassure Scorpio, but Scorpio will probably be looking for more passion at times.

The longer a relationship lasts with a Scorpio, the more secure it tends to become. He is naturally suspicious and Virgo will need to provide a lot of reassurance.

Scorpios carry the deceits of the past with a hurt as fresh as if it was yesterday. Many an ill-mannered Scorpio has bored a first date to tears with vitriolic stories of his ex.

This can turn into full-blown self-pity, which is not attractive to anyone, and poor old Scorpio can become his own worst enemy. A Scorpio is better young and fresh. A Scorpio with baggage is hard to convince, although Virgo can be very convincing.

Yet Scorpios possess bucketloads of passion. You will not find a more passionate sign in the zodiac. Once convinced of the other's commitment and deeply in love, Scorpio will lavish Virgo with flattery and affection, two things that Virgo is quite fond of. The heart of Scorpio is a delicious pool to drown in.

Sex will take compromise, as Virgo doesn't like to get her hands dirty while Scorpio is more primitive and less squeamish. Harmonising your different natures will take some effort, but there is much to be gained from having a go.

The Social Scorpio

Scorpios are generally more your one-on-one type of person. They are happy to go with you to any party and enjoy the refreshments and the entertainment, but they usually want to stick close. At dinner parties, they generally resist group conversation, preferring instead to turn to the person next to them and engage their interest.

Socially, Scorpios like to have a foil for their own personality. A Taurus is perfect for this purpose as they are a diametrically opposite in character because they sit exactly opposite each other on the zodiac wheel. Scorpio's cool intellect is balanced by Taurus' warm conversation; Scorpio's vampish sexuality is juxtaposed with Taurus' homely appearance and so on.

Scorpios are well aware of the intrigue that surrounds them when they play the mysterious lone wolf, but it can be a little lonely if they don't have a trusty friend to help forge the real connections. That is where the foil comes in. Scorpio can continue to appear cool and mysterious, while her erstwhile friend makes sure the invites keep coming and the diary is full.

Super competitive, they will make a game out of any social situation to keep themselves amused. For some, it is snaring the most eligible bachelor in the room, for others it is a bit more risky and involves consuming large amounts of inebriating substances. Drinking games take on a deadly intensity with any Scorpio and should not be entered into by the faint-hearted, although Scorpio is more likely going to be the one to overdo it.

This will happen at least once for every Scorpio. And they usually only do it once because, having discovered their limit, they hate losing control and feel embarrassment with burning intensity. In fact, they are sometimes in danger of reducing their life's experience down to the things that they are pretty sure they have a handle on, so there is no opportunity for getting red in the face.

There is the lone wolf Scorpio, but there is also the zealot groupie Scorpio who throws himself into one cause or another. This is the sign of sex and religion don't forget, so Scorpios are just as likely to get themselves deeply involved in some sort of club-life, whether that be karate, scouting, political activism or the Church of the Latter-Day Motorcycle Rebels. Whatever it is, they will be true converts, running the cake stall and cornering people on the bus, letting them know how much it has changed their life.

And this is true. Scorpio is all about change, the transition from death to life, so Scorpios spend their lives looking for deeper meaning in their existence, evolving this process through many stages, and this includes their social interactions. Scorpio is looking for rebirth in every relationship, no matter how fleeting it may seem.

How to Woo Your Scorpio

If you go to a party together, you need to master the art of letting your Scorpio go and reeling him in. Scorpios generally feel a bit on edge in a social situation with a partner, as they can see too much danger in flirtatious situations and they are very quick to jealousy.

Make sure you have a proprietary hand on the small of their back when you are introducing them to people. Meet their eyes across the room, and if you see they need a drink, get them one.

Break away from the group to go up behind them and whisper in their ear that they look fantastic. You will have the hairs on the back of their neck standing up in excitement.

Gifts for Your Scorpio

Scorpios are intense and passionate, with a love of mystery and secrets. They get as much pleasure wondering what's inside the box as they do opening it.

They love to investigate – think about mysteriously giving them only a clue to the present. For instance, if you are planning on surprising them with a romantic weekend for their birthday (for these sex addicts, this idea will fill them with joy), wrap up a carry-on luggage bag, packed with nothing but black lacy lingerie. Their eyes will sparkle with delight as they put two and two together. It's at that moment you can take the plane tickets out of your top pocket.

Giving the gift in secret will titillate them even more. If you have bought a bracelet for her, wait until you are at a party. Pull her away mysteriously during the evening to somewhere secluded to give her your gift. After a passionate embrace, make a show of going back into the party as if nothing has happened.

Some Scorpios like to flirt with the occult, so they might like a crystal ball, Tarot cards, Rune stones or a book on white magic. Scorpios also love water and they like to swim, so a new swimsuit might be a good idea. Exotic perfumes, satin sheets or something a little kinky will tease their sensual tastes.

SAGITTARIUS/VIRGO

These two make great business partners. Sagittarius keeps the notion of the forest intact, while Virgo considers each individual tree, straightening every bough and sweeping away those pesky leaves.

They will have great success, but some patience is required as they both must realise that their different approaches are completely complementary. If Virgo doesn't roll her eyes at yet another rendition of the ten-year plan and Sagittarius doesn't airily brush off Virgo's petty concerns like, say, where the cash is coming from, the business will surely fly.

As lovers, the compatibility is more difficult. As fellow mutable signs, Virgo and Sagittarius will find joy in communicating with each other, but the stimulating conversation is where the stimulation will end. Sagittarius (especially females) are passionate but physically undemonstrative, and Virgo's cool exterior needs more than a little push by someone very affectionate. This is not a cuddly combination. But, with understanding, Sagittarius can get Virgo to laugh at herself a little more and Virgo can focus some of that Sagittarian energy in productive ways.

Steven Spielberg (Sagittarius) and ex wife, Amy Irving (Virgo), have this combination.

Sagittarians are explorers both of the world and of the mind. They love to travel and experience new people, places and cultures, but they are also happy to sit at home in front of an open fire, glass of red by the hearth, exploring ideas and thoughts with good friends. They generally love to find out about people and explore philosophy with strangers. Sagittarians have been known to take several hours buying a litre of milk after starting up a conversation on the bus or at the local shops.

Sagittarians like to wander, literally and in their minds, and Virgo will accommodate that to a point, although she would much prefer stability. Sagittarius can inadvertently stray, especially if the affair is with someone unusual or famous and thus is an experience that will never be repeated. The cliche about having to always try things once was no doubt made up by a Sagittarian, and this is inclusive of sexual conquests in both male and female.

You will have a lot of fun and enjoy a wonderful life together, but Sagittarius will have to learn to mind his tongue, because his tactless comments can be roundly rebutted by the critical Virgo. Sagittarius can hit his mark with disarming accuracy and even the self-critical Virgo may be surprised at the cruel truth of his jokes.

Virgo is slow to anger, but can be equally cruel with the added dagger of being completely conscious of her sting. It is probably best to save the king hits for the boardroom rather than the bedroom.

The Social Sagittarius

Like Leo, no party is ever big enough for two Sagittarians. If two Sags ever come across each other in a party environment, there is sure to be a showdown, twenty paces at dawn. Only one will survive. At first, the two will circle each other (metaphorically, of course). Sag One tosses in a one-liner. Sag Two recognises an opponent. He smirks, and counters with small joke. Sag One will bide her time, waiting for an opportunity to tell one of her hilarious tales, usually set in a far-off country. Sag Two will brush off this attack with a marvellous rejoinder, something truly pants-wetting, that just happens to be in a country even more remote than the setting for Sag One's vignette. And so on.

Eventually, after at first entertaining, tiring, bewildering and then alienating everyone else in the group with their horsey posturing, everyone will wander off, leaving the Sags locked in a centaur to centaur tussle for supremacy, hysterically countering each other's tall tales with even taller ones. Each Sag needs to prove that they are more funny, more worldly, more spiritual and more well read than the other, completely forgetting that their true aim was to entertain, something that they are both now failing dismally at.

Sad but true. And at least most Sags will admit it, especially after a few lubricating beverages. Whoever made up the saying 'in vino veritas' had just been on the town with a Sagittarian. Sags are happy to spill their guts on most things when stone cold sober. When they have had a few, they are happy to spill everyone else's as well. They have many reasons for doing this and only one of them commendable. They value the truth above everything, and they would never let a secret out that they wouldn't be quite happy to have revealed about themselves. But as I have just pointed out, there are very few things that a Sag will keep hidden in their own closet, so their temperature reading for other people's secrets is usually a good ten degrees cooler than most other people's assessments. The key is, make sure your Sag knows when you are letting them in on a Big One. It won't guarantee that the story will never be told, but at least Sag will have the good grace to feel guilty when they finally do spill it.

Sags don't do anything by halves, so if they are out for a big night on the town, plan for a big morning as well. Their physical stamina is legendary and their enthusiasm unbounded – a lethal combination for most other humanoids. They like to keep the party moving, both conversationally and energy-wise, but they also like to keep everyone moving physically, and they are usually the ones pushing to move on to a nightclub, just when everyone was settling in nicely.

They can be wildly generous or happy to bot freely, especially as they have usually just lost their wallet/car/shirt in some strange-but-true situation that they are bound to bounce back out of, usually with more change in their pocket than before the drama ensued. Their 'easy come, easy go' attitude has been reinforced by years of them falling straight back onto their feet after the most unlikely disasters, so you won't mind if you help them out of this last scrape, will you? You know they're good for it!

How to Woo Your Sagittarius

Intrigue them, surprise them, tantalise them, worry them, just don't ever bore them. You could take Sagittarius just about anywhere for your first date as long as it is just the tiniest bit exotic. McDonald's and a blockbuster movie are not going to do the trick. But a Ninja film and duck soup on formica tables in a café in Chinatown will charm her. If it is a new experience, she will love it whether or not she liked the movie, and she will love debating the merits of Ninja films with you late into the night.

Later on, take her away as often as you can afford it. It doesn't have to be an overnight trip, but springing a surprise flight to the capital city for dinner and a show and a night on the town will delight her. A trip to the coast to fossick about in antique stores or an afternoon at the wineries in the hills will have her glowing. Check out river cruises that might take you to the nearest port for a seafood dinner – such exotic pleasures can be surprisingly affordable.

Gifts for Your Sagittarius

Sagittarians love to give presents as an expression of their warm personality. They usually agonise for weeks over what to buy, and almost always spend an embarrassing amount of money – money is not that important to the Sagittarius, and after all, what price a friend or loved one? Jupiter is the giver of wealth and is associated with prosperity, laughter and happiness, so it's not surprising that Sagittarians are at their best when gifts are being exchanged, such as at Christmas.

Sadly, these gifts are not always on the mark, but they would be mortified if they thought they had got it wrong, so be gentle.

When buying for your Sagittarius, remember they usually feel comforted by their colours indigo and royal purple. Displays of honesty are very important to them, so it really is the thought that counts. If the giver forgets to write a card, then the gift is as good as flawed.

Books always go down well, especially if you have read it so they can discuss it with you later. Clothes are often a nice idea, as they usually can't stand shopping for themselves, and have a very laissez-faire sense of style that will accommodate most things.

Anything that will give them a new experience is accepted with joy: a shiatsu massage (massages are good for Sagittarius as they are generally not physically demonstrative); a hot-air balloon ride; a night out at a cocktail bar trying everything on the menu (they can hold their drink); tickets to a show; or enrolment in a course of life drawing/salsa dancing/theology classes.

CAPRICORN/VIRGO

Wonderfully matched in many ways, this pair may find life a little too serene sometimes, even a little too predictable. Both Virgo and Capricorn prefer the classics, simple elegance and either a very conservative, traditional style or an austere less-is-more, keep-it-simple style. Sometimes, this translates into emotional terms also and you could find yourselves in a rut. A pleasantly serene rut, but a rut all the same.

Hard to believe as you both crave predictability, but you may have to make the effort every now and then to take a little walk on the wild side – provided you are both home for *The Bill* and tucked into bed by 10 o'clock, of course!

That is not to say that this is always the case. Ex couple Gothic rocker Marilyn Manson (Capricorn) and 'Charmed' witchy-poo Rose McGowan (Virgo) are this combination, but you probably tend more towards the traditional romance of a couple like Lauren Bacall (Virgo) and Humphrey Bogart (Capricorn). Annie Lennox (Capricorn) and Dave Stewart (Virgo) from 1980's group the Eurythmics were this pairing.

You are marvellously productive together, Capricorn providing the strategy and Virgo the talent. You can rely on each other for an honest opinion, which makes life much easier and more enjoyable.

Capricorns seem to grow young, rather than grow old. They are born thirty, and spend their youth and early twenties growing their body into its rightful age. Most would love to have skipped all those tiresome early years, having to be friends with immature brats and having no control over their destiny. The teenage years are especially painful for a Capricorn. Teenage rebellion holds no sway with him; he just wants to get out of school, so he can start earning a wage and take some control of his life.

Virgo as also quiet and well behaved as a little one, but is more likely to have had a misspent youth than her Capricorn partner. Both prize fidelity and should have no problems with jealousy. Their ideas on commitment are pretty much in accord. Just remember to mix it up a little every now and then and don't take life too seriously.

The Social Capricorn

Capricorns can't resist using a party or gathering as a business networking opportunity. At least that is how it can come across, before Cap has even had a chance to let his hair down. Poor old Cappie, most things he does are interpreted as something to do with his practical, steadfast, money-hungry and status-thirsty Capricorn side, but it is not always the case. Sometimes Cap can just come across as a little too pressing and a little too forward because he doesn't quite know how to give himself over to the conversation. Is it a crime to ask too many questions? And is it any wonder that he doesn't think his life or his thoughts are remotely conversation worthy? Capricorns are always being told they are terminally boring. Not really a boost to the old self-esteem when you are trying to chat up a pretty lady, is it?

But after Cap has warmed up, and after he has stopped quizzing you on your expected gross output for the financial year to date, he might even reveal a few of his funnier observations on the party at hand. The Cap sense of humour is wry and dry and just a little bit wicked, especially when it comes to summing up a character or a situation in a few funny words. For this reason, they are mostly observers rather than initiators or participators. They will get involved but usually only if they are in total control. They are either standing on the sidelines or running the show. There is no in-between.

And they are fabulous at running the show. Every need will be met, every whim catered for with ruthless efficiency. A Capricorn party is a seamless affair, if a little lacking in imagination. But the drinks are cold, the food is hot, the entertainment starts on time and the speeches are short and sweet – what more could you ask for?

They are loyal and honest friends who enjoy a 'less is more' approach to gathering and keeping friends. They are ambitious in many areas of their life, but they are not usually the type to go and count up their Christmas cards as a booster for their self-esteem. It must have been a Capricorn who said you should only be able to fit your good friends on one hand, otherwise you are spreading yourself too thin.

There is, of course, the other type of Capricorn, the hip as hip rock star Cap whose commanding presence makes everyone else in the room check their cool credentials nervously. Don't forget, David Bowie, Patti Smith, Michael Stipe, Annie Lennox and Janis Joplin are all Capricorns. When you think Capricorn, you also think independent, powerful, seriously charismatic, and never too eager to please. These guys demand an entourage of adoring fans just for waking up in the morning. If your Capricorn friend happens to be more rock star than rookie, you have got yourself a goldmine of invites and open doors. These Caps are usually way too cool to truly take advantage of freebies, so you can make yourself a nice little social life using up Cap's unused drink cards or passes to this and that.

How to Woo Your Capricorn

Dress well, for goodness sake, and check that your nails are clean. Capricorn does not demand a great beauty, but he does look for taste and grooming. If you are arranging the restaurant, choose somewhere with an established reputation, and an even better wine list. Capricorn won't quibble about the prices but he knows good service, so you don't want to risk a new restaurant.

He will love talking about his work and family, but you may wonder after a while if he wants to know anything about you. Of course he does, he just doesn't want to be impertinent about how he asks. Sometimes Capricorn is so uptight about manners that he can seem quite rude. Gently introduce yourself into the conversation and you will see his interest pick up. Be sure to put in a few points about your breeding, for example that your grandfather fought in World War II. Leave out that your Dad dodged the draft by engaging in the longest-running arts degree ever recorded by a university, at least for now.

Take mental notes on the hobbies of his mother and sisters. Down the track you can please him no end by taking his mother out for shopping and coffee. He probably still lives with her, so you are going to get to know her pretty well anyway.

Gifts for Your Capricorn

Practical, sturdy, lasts forever. Go all-out on the quality of a gift, but don't buy brand names unless you want to hear snorts of derision.

Capricorns like homewares and tools, but they also like to be treated as though they have interests other than the practical. It may seem strange, but Capricorn will not hesitate to buy herself whatever she needs, even though she will never buy those things that she might whimsically wish for. Capricorn does not put a high enough price on her own happiness, so it is up to her friends and loved ones to litter her life with frivolity.

Capricorns love a gift that has taken a lot of time and patience to make. Their colour preferences are indigo, dark brown and black. But the key word, whatever you buy, is quality.

AQUARIUS/VIRGO

There is good mental rapport here. Virgo focuses on specific details and prefers to specialise in a certain area, while Aquarius takes a wider, more global view and looks for interrelationships in a large system.

You will fascinate each other with your disparity of ideas

and spend hours picking each other's brains for gems of inspiration. You won't agree on anything, but neither takes an intellectual argument personally so this is not a problem.

These are two fairly stand-offish signs and the Aquarius aloofness (so appealing in the early days) may become a problem. Your physical relationship may be a bit cool or formal. Hopefully there are other astrological factors to provide warmth, affection and romantic attraction.

Cameron Diaz (Virgo) and Matt Dillon (Aquarius) were of this pairing, as was the very short-lived marriage of Hollywood royalty Lisa Marie Presley (Aquarius) to Nicolas Cage (Virgo). Lisa Marie also married another Virgo Michael Jackson.

Aquarius can't stand commitment and will do anything to get out of confirming a date or committing to a time. If you invite an Aquarian friend out to dinner on Friday night, no matter how far in advance you ask, don't expect an answer until Friday morning. Don't ever ask for a time. Even if they volunteer one, it will bear no relation to the actual time that they arrive.

Aquarians are radicals; they like to think outside the square and the box it came in as well. They have to allow for any unforseen variables – what if a better offer came along?

Virgo prefers her diary dates to be cut and dried weeks ahead of time. She likes to know where she will be at any given time, with a generous allowance for error. When going to see a show, Virgo likes to be there at least half an hour before, to pick up the tickets and establish where to put her coat. She has been known to take a little reconnaissance tour before big events, just so she can feel at ease. I knew one Virgo who liked to have a look in the bathroom when we arrived at a venue, whether she needed to go or not. She just liked to know where it was so she could relax.

This is hilarious to Aquarius, who arrives at a show as the curtain rises, butting out his cigarette and signalling goodbye to someone he met on the walk up to the theatre. He slinks into the back row and makes his opening observations. If you are unlucky enough to be sitting next to him, he will whisper a prediction about where the plot might be going – 'I bet she is a man...', that sort of thing. More infuriating is that he is always right!

Aquarians love the idea of people, but as long as it is only people in the abstract; they get a little squeamish about the reality. They may love the idea of living in a commune, but the reality of living with someone else's less-than-sanitary habits can be too much. Virgos are of a similar bent, although they are scrupulously clean and will pick the hairs out of the shower, especially if they have to shower in it. This is a hygienic match.

The Social Aquarius

Socially, Aquarians are more likely to be keeping the wheels turning at any gathering than being a mere mingling cog. They are the sign of universal gatherings, so they are often the organisers rather than the life of the party.

This suits their keenly observant personality down to the ground. They would much rather have the odd bemusing conversation with the flotsam to judge the temperature of a party, than be forced to be the star of the group. That doesn't mean they are not capable of 'holding court'. In fact, when they deign to dazzle you with their brilliance, you can be sure their light will outshine even the most riotous Leo – but they would usually prefer if you did the talking. You reveal more of yourself that way.

You can pick any Aquarius on the dance floor by their unusual dress and their decidedly different moves. Not for them the 'step-together, step-together' with a 'white-man's overbite'. No, if Aquarius is going to shake their booty, you can be sure they will be moving to a different drum than the rest of the crowd. They are usually well aware of the sort of impression they are giving to others, so they won't embarrass themselves with any unsavoury dance techniques, but they will get themselves noticed.

If your Aquarian friend decides to really break out and indulge in a few beverages, the quiet and thoughtful veneer is soon shed. Don't forget that the Aquarian motto is 'I know'. They can go from delicately teasing out everyone's opinions one minute to boorishly dominating conversation with their own political beliefs the next.

But usually they are a paragon of moderacy. Besides, they enjoy psychoanalysis too much to give that up!

They are not loyal to any one place, and are unlikely to have a local drinking haunt. Rather, they like to go where things are happening, so they are usually up on the latest clubs and bars around town, although preferably away from the mainstream. They generally enjoy music or theatre or both, so they can be a bit of a walking, talking gig guide, but be prepared for anything if you take them up on one of their suggestions. The Aquarian idea of a nice night at the theatre is more likely to contain interpretative dance and full-frontal nudity than your run-of-the-mill production of *The King and I*.

In a party situation, Aquarians are natural flirts but in a combative way. Flattery is not usually a tool of choice, in fact, most Aquarians feel more comfortable when they have riled up the object of their affections and they are engaged in an intellectual tussle. This unusual strategy can have surprisingly good results and can also get Aquarius over the next hurdle – the physical. Aquarius is not a very touchy-feely sign and they are much more comfortable putting you in a playful headlock than a romantic clinch, at least for now. In summary, being wooed by an Aquarian can feel a little like being teased by your best friend's older brother.

How to Woo Your Aquarius
Approach from the side, never head on, as there is nothing that will scare an Aquarian off more than a full-frontal romance attack. They can't stand romantic nonsense like roses and candlelight, which they see as so predictable, tacky and unimaginative.

At this point, rose wilting pathetically, you may just want to put down your heart-shaped box of chocolates and run.

No one would blame you. Not even Aquarius would blame you, and they will probably be quite remorseful next time they see you, once they've had a chance to calm down.

It is not that Aquarius really thinks you have no imagination (although she does love things to be a little bit unusual), she just got a bit of a shock. You were thinking of a nice night out, all she saw was a marriage proposal and a mortgage and a dozen snotty-nosed kids. The bars clanged down around her. She felt short of breath, claustrophobic, so she shot out the worst insult in her repertoire – that you are ordinary.

Now, what you have to do is very simple. Be her friend. But not just any old friend, make sure you are the wittiest and most intelligent friend on the planet, with a hint of mystery about you. Engage, intrigue, woo her all at the same time. Walk away. Let some time pass, hold out for several weeks if you can. Then 'bump' into her; make an impression, make lots of eye contact and then make an excuse. Get out of there. Then the next day, send her a little gift, something really unusual, with no subtext of romance.

You must have her thinking that she is the one doing the wooing and that you are the one playing hard to get. This goes double-plus if the Aquarian is male. Whatever you do, attack from left of field – they can fall in love, and they make wonderful, stable, faithful partners who are never short on conversation once in love; you just have to convince them it is their idea.

Aquarians are also not adverse to email. This is another way of casually engaging their attention and showing off your witty repartee.

Gifts for Your Aquarius

Aquarians generally like unusual or quirky gifts. But quirky should not be read as 'whacky'. And Aquarians hate anything that is crude or rude.

For something unusual, head to any antiques shop or second-hand bookshop and it will be full of stuff for your

Aquarian. Ancient Tibetan mountain bells, a shoe snob, a collection of *Boy's Annuals* from the 1950s, a barber's clock that tells the time in mirror image – you get the idea. If it makes you stop and muse, 'isn't that unusual?', you are probably on the right track.

The Aquarian's colour is aqua. They may not wear it, but they seem to have it around, even more so than other signs and their colours, often in their bedroom colour schemes.

Some Aquarians like techno gadgets, the newer the better. A wrist-watch mobile telephone will elicit a squeal of delight. Others are on a more humanitarian and environmental bent, and will like anything you buy from Greenpeace, Oxfam or Community Aid Abroad. Don't forget your Aquarian when travelling. That is the perfect time to stock up on one-of-a-kinds.

PISCES/VIRGO

Virgo loves analysing and Pisces loves to dream. These two sit on opposite ends of the zodiac, which usually means a strong instantaneous sexual attraction, eyes across the room, love at first sight.

Opposites of the zodiac often make successful couples, even though at first glance they may not seem to have much in common. In fact, all opposites come from compatible elemental groups (fire/air or earth/water) and all are of the same quadruplicity (cardinal, fixed or mutable), so they are more compatible than someone of the sign before or after the opposite.

Ambiguity is the bane of Virgo's existence and she will go out of her way to quash it, or at least file it neatly in a folder marked 'To be reconciled later'.

Pisces wallows in ambiguity and is quite content to absorb lots of contradictory ideas. Virgo likes to carve out a niche, developing expertise in a defined domain, whereas Pisces drifts among a wider variety of interests. Virgo likes neat and tidy, Pisces loves a bit of clutter. Pisces is poetry to Virgo's facts.

Oh, it all sounds too hard doesn't it? But the truth is your differences do not necessarily conflict with each other; neither of you is ambitious or egocentric; you are both gentle, even shy people, and your sensitivity is a plus in this relationship.

Virgo will have to take the reins a little, whether male or female. Piscean women like to be romanced and taken care of. She might put up a protest, but only because she thinks you may be a modern man who would like to hear it.

It is the same for the Pisces male. Let a Pisces man open doors and buy you dinner and generally think he is the tough one. He needs to wear this mask society taught him to wear as a little boy – because boys don't cry. But before long, he will be writing you poetry, getting clucky over pictures of baby animals and bawling his eyes out with you when you're sad.

Keep the first date fairly formal. Pisces loves to dress up and will be disappointed if she can't wow you with her make-up and her clothes. The less relaxed the better; Pisces prefer to wear the masks of formality.

Pisceans are careful about expressing their feelings as their emotions are very important to them. Feelings are not in the driving seat for Virgo (the intellect is), but she does know how to treat someone well and will take care of Pisces in the way that Pisces needs. Some find Pisces' neediness too clingy, but Virgo can handle with care. This is a loving match.

The Social Pisces

Pisces are either on or off. There is no denying that. Some days they have all the energy in the world to give to a social situation. Other days, not even Dr Phil could get a coherent response from them. They only have so much energy to give, and once it is used up, it is like trying to start a car with a flat battery. You just can't.

So don't take it personally if your Pisces friend is a little, well, mute at your next party. Yours is probably the last in a line of a few social engagements and they just don't have any more talk left in them. Resist the temptation to make them feel just a teensy bit bad about being such a wet mop, because they are already berating themselves like crazy and growing mildly depressed about their inability to muster up the required energy.

When they are on top of the world, their dreamy storytelling and eccentricities have them charming everybody in the room. Despite their ancient countenance, they are surprisingly easy to kid and they often fall prey to other people's more wicked sense of humour. In the dictionary, the word gullible should be illustrated with a little fish.

Pisces are much better in one-on-one situations when their thoughtful and intuitive responses are able to be honed in one direction. They tell a whimsy story, often picking out the most unusual details to colour their tale to very good effect.

You can sometimes get the impression that your Pisces friend is lasting out the conversation with you out of a sense of obligation and this can be for two reasons.

The first is because Pisces often doesn't know how to end an interaction, even when they really should be leaving soon/putting on the dinner/getting back to work. They will often just sound more and more distracted and strained until you put them out of their misery and declare that you really should be off now.

The other is much more spiritual and more to do with their life journey than you. Pisces just tend to feel like a) they have tonnes more time on their hands than the rest of us (after all, this is at least their twelfth time around on the planet) and b) there is nothing much that hasn't been said before and nothing that you have to say will have a lot of impact on them or the world. This can manifest itself into an amused, if not just a wee bit smug, smile that speaks volumes. It says, 'Come now little whippersnapper, why worry now? It will happen one day, if not in this lifetime, then the next.'

They can throw a surprisingly good party though, because it gives them the inflexibility of a fixed deadline to work to. Pisces are notorious procrastinators and will find any little loophole to exploit when trying to push out a timeline, but a party date is much more difficult to chop and change. Pisces will usually rise to this challenge and put in the effort to make their preparations orderly and logical, as opposed to their usual preparatory style, which is distracted and dithering. Their fertile imagination makes sure the affair will be a little different from the norm and that everyone will be talking about the night for weeks to come.

How to Woo Your Pisces

Pisces women are old-fashioned ladies at heart, and don't let them tell you any different. The odd one will attempt to put up the modern woman front, but she will turn to mush if you run around and open the car door for her. Treat her like she is the most precious and delicate flower you ever came across, and she will melt right there in front of you.

They will probably be nervous, so you might have to take the reins of the conversation for the first half-hour or so (this is not always true, some Pisces come into their own in romance and will be quite aggressive in their flirting). A night at the theatre or the ballet and they will be in their element. A nice idea for a daytime date is 'high tea' at a posh hotel. It's all marvellously civilised and a lot of fun. Pisces love play-acting at being posh.

Once things get a little more intimate, make any excuse to give her a foot massage. Pisceans completely bliss out as soon as you touch their feet.

Gifts for Your Pisces

Because Pisces sometimes have to be forced into doing things for themselves, and are also notorious for ignoring their health, consider a voucher for a relaxation massage or a paid-up course in tai chi.

If your Pisces is the self-destructive type, stay away from presents of alcohol, but a great fantasy novel or a fantasy computer game will thrill them. Don't expect to see them for the next couple of days, though.

Pisces are soppy old sentimentalists for the most part, so frame a wedding photo of their grandparents or their parents or arrange a slide night for them – really rummage around in the box for some unusual old slides. Set the atmosphere with some well-chosen music. They will be misty-eyed and reaching for the tissues by the end of it.

If you have been away for some time and have received letters from them (Pisceans are fantastic letter writers, but terrible emailers), make them dinner and read through the letters over a bottle of red wine. This is a blue-ribbon winner with the nostalgic Pisces.

They like trinkets and old-fashioned things. Piscean women retain their girly quality throughout their lives. A music box or a china doll or teddy bear with the scent of eras past always goes down well.

Anything to encourage the considerable creative talents of Pisces is great, but getting them to sit down to do it in between all their commitments to other people is another thing. This is why booking them into a course like painting is for their own good, as they will have to go and enjoy it because they are doing it for you! They also particularly like gifts associated with water.

OTHER COMPATIBILITIES

ARIES/ARIES
Temper tantrums erupt into major wars. Only one party can win and you both hate defeat. Hot and fiery.

ARIES/TAURUS
Taureans make money. Aries spend it; so the Bull toils diligently without seeing the fruits of her labour. Compromise is a must.

ARIES/GEMINI
A wonderful alliance. This is an exciting, sexual encounter that (dare I say it) can last! So spontaneous there is no time for boredom.

ARIES/CANCER

The Crab is far too sensitive and slow for Aries' tempestuous nature. Aries has difficulty listening to the Crab's negativity. Tolerance is the key.

ARIES/LEO

Exhilaration plus. Sharing the same likes and dislikes you lead a charmed life, searching out excitement, love, laughs and fun.

ARIES/LIBRA

Aries can't tell his claret from his beaujolais, and lacks sophistication. Libra is too lazy for speedy Aries. Fun while it lasts.

ARIES/SCORPIO

A hot and heavy union, but too hot to handle for the carefree Aries as the possessive Scorpio will give you a short leash.

ARIES/SAGITTARIUS

You are both fun-loving people and oblivious to the faults in each other that might drive other people loopy. Laughter and love.

ARIES/CAPRICORN

Aries can spend it as fast as the Goat can make it, which drives the bean-counting Capricorn to despair. Compromise.

ARIES/AQUARIUS

Great conversation and a good game of chess; however, this time Aries is the one guessing. Who will call who, and when? Interesting.

ARIES/PISCES

The Fish will find Aries; intellectualising superficial and Aries will find the Piscean emotional games exhausting.

TAURUS/TAURUS

Same-sign relationships are always trying. However you make a welcoming home, and will put on scrumptious dinner parties.

TAURUS/GEMINI

Taurus will find Gemini like holding onto a handful of dry sand. Geminis don't mentally sit down for one minute, Taurus loves to muse.

TAURUS/CANCER

Pure bliss! Cancer makes a good home and gives physical affection, which is all Taurus wants. Sensual heaven on earth. A lovely match.

TAURUS/LEO

Great sex appeal, magnanimous Leo will shower Taurus with the finer things in life. Longevity, stability and loyalty. Worth a red-hot go.

TAURUS/LIBRA

Venus rules both these signs and gives their pairing harmony. Pots of money required to appease their desire for luxury.

TAURUS/SCORPIO

Taurus must appear to be wholly and solely committed at all times. In the long run, this can wear thin, even for the diligent Bull.

TAURUS/SAGITTARIUS

Two very different life philosophies. Both must agree that no way is the better way, and to love each other for it.

TAURUS/CAPRICORN

Capricorn will be aloof at first, but the warm rays of Venus will soon melt the exterior of caution in the Goat.

TAURUS/AQUARIUS
If you seem like you are from opposite sides of the planet, that is because you are. A similar sense of humour may see you through.

TAURUS/PISCES
Taurus' practicality can comfort the emotional Pisces. Pisces allows earth-bound Taurus to dream a little. Usually a joy.

GEMINI/GEMINI
Frenetic is one word to describe this pair. Life is so far into the fast lane they will have to build a bypass.

GEMINI/CANCER
Cancer fulfils Gemini's physical needs, Gemini brightens Cancer's world, but Gemini's flirting will wound Cancer. Be wary.

GEMINI/LEO
Affectionate but constantly upstaging each other at parties, they both love to see the funny side of their dramatic coupling. A dinner-party duo.

GEMINI/LIBRA
Love is in the air! Affectionate, seeks fun, and loves to entertain and travel. Neither is jealous or demanding.

GEMINI/SCORPIO
Scorpio is inflexible, Gemini is fickle. Gemini loves people, Scorpio likes privacy. Be careful with one another.

GEMINI/SAGITTARIUS
A wild ride, Gemini and Sagittarius sit opposite in the zodiac and will enjoy picking over each other's brains. An oxygen-fed house on fire.

GEMINI/CAPRICORN

Capricorn needs walls and floors, while Gemini likes open air; Capricorn worries about security, Gemini worries about losing freedom.

GEMINI/AQUARIUS

As inconsistent as each other, a taste for the bizarre and new people unites them. Gemini seeks knowledge, Aquarius has it.

GEMINI/PISCES

Gemini is attracted to Pisces' dreamy nature, but Gemini's thoughtlessness will bruise Pisces' spirit. Persistence.

CANCER/CANCER

Sensual bedmates, both are too sensitive, too demanding and in need of an enormous amount of reassurance.

CANCER/LEO

Cancer might shy from Leo's exuberance but like the moon reflects the sun, you can both feed each other's good qualities.

CANCER/LIBRA

Cancer seeks emotional partnering, Libra seeks intellectual communion. Sexual rapport is not affectionate enough for Cancer.

CANCER/SCORPIO

Both value emotional commitment and Cancer's sensuality ignites Scorpio's passion. Together they build a love cocoon with intimacy, intensity and depth.

CANCER/SAGITTARIUS

Cancer's imagination complements Sagittarius' worldly knowledge, but better friends than lovers. Cancer needs reassurance, which is a Sagittarius blindspot.

CANCER/CAPRICORN
Cancer plays sensitive flower to Capricorn's domineering protector. Adjustments have to be made, but worth the effort.

CANCER/AQUARIUS
Cancer needs security; Aquarius is a lone wolf who, if trapped, will gobble up Cancer's warm, responsive nature. Not a great idea.

CANCER/PISCES
Pisces love protective Cancer, and Cancer loves having someone to love, especially the emotionally responsive Pisces. A nurturing match.

LEO/LEO
Cooperation. Ah, yes, not something that comes easily to either of you. Like two king lions in a pride, you can expect to butt heads a little.

LEO/LIBRA
These two will enjoy fabulous sex romps, but when it finally gets down to the nitty-gritty of commitment, there may be some problems.

LEO/SCORPIO
A clash of wills. Mutual attraction to strength of character adds to the conquest, but once caught that proud, stubborn streak gets up your left nostril.

LEO/SAGITTARIUS
Sagittarius will keep introducing new ideas and experiences to keep Leo from getting into a rut. Sagittarius adds the humour and Leo adds the panache. A good match.

LEO/CAPRICORN
Leo's gaudy temperament clashes with Capricorn's refined colour scheme. Leos are bombastic when it comes to intellectual detail, which irritates Capricorn.

LEO/AQUARIUS
Leo loves the world and Aquarius loves humanity. Leo loves a good surprise and Aquarius can provide. Fun.

LEO/PISCES
Leo will never have to vie for the spotlight with Pisces, but Leo can trample Pisces' feelings. Leo finds Pisces too clingy and stifling.

LIBRA/LIBRA
For both of you, your feelings seem real when you share the experience. You invest enormous energy into personal relationships. Harmony and balance.

LIBRA/SCORPIO
Scorpio has an urge to merge, Libra likes to keep a sense of proportion. An interesting match.

LIBRA/SAGITTARIUS
A party duo, outgoing and friendly, Sagittarius provides the grandiose ideas, Libra puts them into perspective.

LIBRA/CAPRICORN
Capricorn can keep Libra in the style to which she is accustomed, Libra can infuse some wine and laughter into Capricorn's orderly life.

LIBRA/AQUARIUS
Great mates with a lust for conversation. You both like things pretty breezy, Aquarius more so than Libra. To the happy couple.

LIBRA/PISCES
Affectionate, creative, artistic both, this is a romantic couple, but Pisces won't find emotional support in Libra and Libra won't find the luxury she craves.

SCORPIO/SCORPIO
Whoa baby, this is intense. Scorpios are all or nothing, so this must be all. Stormy fights and sizzling reunions typify your relationship.

SCORPIO/SAGITTARIUS
Sagittarius feels Scorpio is a dead weight, Scorpio (correctly) suspects Sagittarius doesn't care as much. Sagittarius doesn't have the capacity for Scorpio's depth of feeling.

SCORPIO/CAPRICORN
Naturally suspicious, neither of you is flippant about affection. There is no froth and bubble here – but you don't want that anyway.

SCORPIO/AQUARIUS
Scorpio needs to possess the person and Aquarius wants to own the world, but these two desires are not mutually exclusive. A taste for the unusual.

SCORPIO/PISCES
Scorpio's jealousy makes Pisces feel loved and Pisces' dependency is Scorpio's strength. Communication is on a sensual, unspoken level. Heaven on earth.

SAGITTARIUS/SAGITTARIUS
Unparalleled lust for life, the camaraderie between you is infectious. Guard against superficiality, things might fizzle into just good friends

SAGITTARIUS/CAPRICORN
Optimism and faith versus realism and doubt. Capricorn finds Sagittarius' plans amusing, Sagittarius finds that reaction just a little bit patronising. Worth it.

SAGITTARIUS/AQUARIUS
Friendly but somewhat detached, this will worry neither of

you. A fashionable partnering, you will always know what is up. Enjoyable and interesting.

SAGITTARIUS/PISCES

Lusty, but Pisces is a dreamer not a doer, which will frustrate Sagittarius no end. Sagittarius' sharp tongue will puncture Pisces' dream bubble.

CAPRICORN/CAPRICORN

Stability and love in abundance but light and laughter could be lacking, so have kids, the more the merrier. A long and fruitful love.

CAPRICORN/AQUARIUS

Capricorn brings tenacity and reliability. Aquarius brings ingenuity and sensitivity to current trends. Some warmth and sexual spark makes an interesting match.

CAPRICORN/PISCES

Like a puzzle, these two personalities fill in the weaknesses of the other. Capricorn makes the decisions, Pisces brings the romance. One-plus-one unites.

AQUARIUS/AQUARIUS

Friends or lovers – can lovers still be friends? Of course! You both cry. What happens when lovers are only friends? Hmmm. Softness required.

AQUARIUS/PISCES

Sexually, this is fun, but sex is never enough to keep Aquarius interested. Pisces will struggle to communicate subtle emotional undertones. Not a happy story.

PISCES/PISCES

Eventually you are both going to have to open the shutters and face the real world. One of you must pay the bills – which one is it going to be?